# Setting Priorities in the Age of Austerity

## British, French, and German Experiences

Michael Shurkin

Prepared for the United States Army

The research described in this report was sponsored by the United States Army under contract No. W74V8H-06-C-0001.

**Library of Congress Cataloging-in-Publication Data**

Shurkin, Michael Robert.
  Setting priorities in the age of austerity : British, French, and German experiences / Michael Shurkin.
    p cm
  Includes bibliographical references.
  ISBN 978-0-8330-8039-4 (pbk. : alk. paper)
  1. Great Britain. Army—Appropriations and expenditures. 2. France. Armée—Appropriations and expenditures.
  3. Germany. Heer—Appropriations and expenditures. 4. Great Britain. Army—Organization. 5. France.
  Armée—Organization. 6. Germany. Heer—Organization. 7. Great Britain. Army—Operational readiness.
  8. France. Armée—Operational readiness. 9. Germany. Heer—Operational readiness. I. Title.

  UA649.S54 2013
  355.6'22--dc23

                                                                                          2013016139

The RAND Corporation is a nonprofit institution that helps improve policy and decisionmaking through research and analysis. RAND's publications do not necessarily reflect the opinions of its research clients and sponsors.

**RAND**˚ is a registered trademark.

Published 2013 by the RAND Corporation
1776 Main Street, P.O. Box 2138, Santa Monica, CA 90407-2138
1200 South Hayes Street, Arlington, VA 22202-5050
4570 Fifth Avenue, Suite 600, Pittsburgh, PA 15213-2665
RAND URL: http://www.rand.org/
To order RAND documents or to obtain additional information, contact
Distribution Services: Telephone: (310) 451-7002;
Fax: (310) 451-6915; Email: order@rand.org

# Preface

The purpose of this paper is to provide insights regarding British, French, and German approaches to managing significant military budget cuts while sustaining their commitment to retaining a full spectrum of army capabilities and maintaining a high state of readiness for at least a significant portion of their forces. Specifically, this project looks at the choices they are making with respect to how they spend dwindling resources: What force structure do they identify as optimal? How much readiness do they regard as necessary? Which capabilities do they abandon? It turns out that all three armies remain nominally committed to full-spectrum capabilities. However, looking closely at their emerging force structure and their efforts to elaborate doctrines that match their understanding of the role of the military in future conflicts (i.e., what they need to be ready for) it is clear that they are, to varying degrees and in different ways, backing away from full spectrum operations (FSO), adopting more tailored force structures, and embracing more nuanced approaches to readiness.

Behind the three armies' choices are assessments of the probability of future conflict based on their reading of recent conflicts, particularly the conflict in Afghanistan and the 2006 Lebanon War. Afghanistan has also played an important role, for example, in why the French army has been able to move forward with its Future Combat Systems–like modernization program, while the UK's comparable program has stalled. Another difference emerges with regard to culture: Some armies simply take the prospect of fighting wars more seriously.

This report should be of particular interest to those concerned with the evolution of U.S. allies' capabilities, as well as to planners thinking about how to prioritize investments in military capabilities in light of dwindling resources. In a sense, others have done this before us.

This paper is based primarily on a close review of key British, French, and German government documents, as well as articles written by military officers that appeared in official and semi-official military publications and the British, French, and German press. The nature of these sources prevented a more-detailed analysis of specific capabilities and weapon systems. All translations are our own. The information reflects the situation as of March 2013.

This research was sponsored by the Assistant Deputy Chief of Staff for Programs, G-8, and conducted within the RAND Arroyo Center's Force Development and Technology Program. The RAND Arroyo Center, part of the RAND Corporation, is a federally funded research and development center sponsored by the United States army.

For additional information on this report, contact the author, Michael Shurkin, mshurkin@rand.org, 703-413-1100 x5947 or Christopher G. Pernin, Director of the Force Development and Technology Program, pernin@rand.org, 703-413-1100 x5197.

# Table of Contents

# Figures

# Tables

# Summary

This report describes how British, French, and German governments and militaries approach the challenge of cutting their defense budgets while preserving their armies' capabilities and maintaining high states of readiness. They are attempting to preserve as much of the spectrum of capabilities as possible by wringing as many efficiencies as they can out of their defense establishment, prioritizing some capabilities while letting others decline to what they assess to be the minimum level required. They are also rebalancing their force structure around new fleets of medium-weight, high-tech armored vehicles in an effort to find a "sweet spot" that will allow them to handle as much of the spectrum of conflict as possible. Finally, they are, to varying degrees, embracing tiered readiness or finding ways to provide graduated levels of readiness within a force generation cycle.

The British Army has been the most adversely effected by the Afghanistan mission and has also been subject to significant budget cuts. British planners believe the army has become too "bespoke" as a result of the particular requirements of the Afghanistan mission and want to restore the army's full spectrum of capabilities. They assess that the optimal way of accomplishing this would be to accept large cuts to the size of the force, embrace specialization by dividing the force into a medium-weight conventional force and a lighter force geared toward missions such as stabilization operations, and adopt a modified form of tiered readiness. They are also hoping to maximize the effectiveness of their reduced conventional forces by introducing a new family of medium-armored vehicles. These vehicles, however, will not enter into service in significant numbers for another decade because the program has been postponed, in part, as a result of the diversion of funds to the Afghanistan mission.

The French military is similarly dedicated to retaining full-spectrum capabilities. Less effected by the Afghanistan mission, the French army is well on its way toward a medium-weight force organized around two new families of high-tech, medium-armor vehicles, the first of which, an Infantry Fighting Vehicle (IFV), is entering service now, and the second of which, an Armored Personnel Carrier (APC), is still in development and on track to be procured soon. The French army has also made the most progress toward fielding what, in the United States, was called Future Combat Systems and is proceeding on schedule with further development and deployment. France has, for example, already fielded squad-level systems in Afghanistan that link individual soldiers to one another and to the new IFVs. France also has folded its heavy assets into two heavy cavalry brigades reserved for high-intensity maneuver warfare. Unlike the British planners, the French military is wary of the proposition that enhancements in quality brought about by technology can substitute for reduced force size. This suggests that, faced with having to make more cuts, the army would prefer to shed capabilities or opt for cheaper but less sophisticated systems for the sake of maintaining its size. It remains to be seen whether the unfolding events in Mali will effect French planning in any way. A new *Livre Blanc* (White Book) laying out defense priorities for the next five years will reveal if the French intend to change their approach, however new cuts appear unlikely at least for the coming fiscal year.

The German military has been subject to significant cuts while attempting to reform itself into a more expeditionary force akin to the French military. The most important change to the German military has been the abandonment of conscription—with the last class of draftees entering the ranks this year. In addition, the German army is following the trend of embracing a medium-weight force built around new APCs and IFVs, believing that it provides the most "bang for the buck" and is the most capable of meeting a broad range of contingencies. The German army is retaining heavy forces, but it is reducing their size and marginalizing them. On paper, the resulting force resembles the French army. However, available evidence suggests that, due to cultural and other factors, including the legal framework in which the military operates, Germany's commitment to the combined-arms maneuver warfare end of the capability spectrum is the weakest of the three militaries discussed in this report. It is instead sliding toward a focus on stability operations while the French try to dig into a middle ground.

# Acknowledgements

The author would like to thank Chris Pernin, of the RAND Corporation, for his guidance and support, as well as David Johnson and Stuart Johnson for sharing their insights on military matters. Special thanks go to Colonel Bertrand Darras, Lt. Colonel Seven de Kerros, Bastien Irondelle, Philippe Gros, Thomas Rid, and Martin Zapfe for sharing with me their knowledge of the French and German militaries, and to Stuart Johnson and Hans Binnendijk for reviewing the report.

# Abbreviations

| | |
|---|---|
| AAB | Air Assault Brigade |
| AFV | armored fighting vehicle |
| AIB | Armoured Infantry Brigade |
| APC | armored personnel carrier |
| ARFORGEN | Army Force Generation |
| BMS | Battlefield Management System |
| FÉLIN | *Fantassin à Equipements et Liaisons Intégrés* [Infantry Soldier with Integrated Equipment and Networks] |
| FRES | Future Rapid Effect System |
| FSO | full spectrum operations |
| GCV | Ground Combat Vehicle |
| HDv | *Heeresdienstvorschrift* |
| IdZ | *Infanterist der Zukunft* [Future Infantryman] |
| IFV | infantry fighting vehicle |
| ISAF | International Security Assistance Force |
| MBT | main battle tank |
| MCP | *Mise en condition avant projection* [Pre-Deployment Training] |
| MoD | Ministry of Defense |
| MRAP | Mine Resistant Ambush Protected |
| NATO | North Atlantic Treaty Organization |
| PEGP | *Politique d'emploi et de gestion des parcs* |
| PPV | protected patrol vehicles |
| PzDiv | *Panzerdivision* [Armored Division] |
| PzGren | *Panzergrenadierdivizion* [Mechanized Infantry] |
| SCORPION | *Synergie du Contact Renforcé par la Polyvalence et l'infovalorisation* [System of Contact Reinforced by Versatility and Information] |
| SDSR | Strategic Defense and Security Review |
| WFM | Whole Fleet Management |
| VAB | *Véhicle de l'Avant Blindée* |
| VBCI | *Véhicule blindé de combat d'infanterie* |
| VBMR | *Véhicule blindé multi-rôles* |

# 1. Introduction

This study examines how the British, French, and German armies are responding to significant budget cuts imposed on them by their governments. The purpose is to derive insight from the evolution of Europe's most important armies' capabilities and the thinking behind the compromises they are making as they set spending priorities according to their understanding of risk and the future role of their armies in military conflict. As looming budget cuts in the United States spur debate about spending priorities and future conflict, the U.S. military can benefit not just from tracking what its strongest allies can and cannot do but also by observing how they have projected future defense needs. The focus of this report is less on specific capabilities than on how these militaries are prioritizing between capabilities and readiness and how they are designing their reduced force structures to match what they assess to be their role in future conflicts. This assessment reflects their understanding of risk and national policy, as well as their conclusions regarding what capabilities they will need versus what capabilities they would like to have. Thus, this study sheds light on the capabilities of British, French, and German armies and provides insights regarding how the U.S. Army might reduce its force structure if required by budgetary limitations.

The armies of our most potent European allies have reached a point where they can no longer be everything they want to be. Like a tank designer's need to choose among the infamous "iron triangle" of protection, firepower, and mobility—as no single platform can provide optimal levels of all three—the British, French, and German armies have found that they must compromise on some combination of capability, sustainability, and readiness. To minimize risk, they are basing these decisions as much as possible on their assessment of the requirements of future conflict.

This study began by attempting to answer two seemingly simple questions: Were the British, French, and German armies abandoning any capabilities? If so, how did they assess risk? Our research found that the three armies insist ostensibly on remaining capable of full spectrum operations (FSO), ranging from disaster relief to high-intensity combined arms maneuver warfare. Indeed, until very recently, they were attempting to maintain the status quo by squeezing what savings they could out of their operating expenses, primarily by reducing their numbers of uniformed and civilian personnel, closing many domestic and overseas facilities, and reorganizing.

However, close examination of British, French, and German plans indicates that they are redefining FSO to encompass a narrower range of capabilities while simultaneously compromising on sustainability and readiness. Britain is trimming its capabilities while—in the hope of holding on to as much as possible—compromising significantly on sustainability and embracing a tiered readiness system that presupposes the avoidance of having to engage in, let

1

alone sustain, an operation of any significant size. Mindful of Israel's experience in Lebanon, the UK strives to retain a conventional capability and thus does not wish to slide further toward a lighter force structure, but it is paying a price in terms of size and sustainability. Germany, in its push to gear its entire military for expeditionary operations, is drifting toward the stability operations side of the spectrum of conflict, in part because of cuts that affect its capacity to conduct higher intensity operations but also because of its own uncertainty about the precise purpose of the German army.

In contrast, France—which suffers from no such confusion—continues to take seriously the prospect of going to war against conventional opponents while remaining committed to conducting multiple stability operations. The French view of stability operations in light of their experience in Afghanistan emphasizes the potential for such fights to spike in intensity. This view validates the continued requirement for conventional skills. France also has a force generation scheme much like the U.S. Army's current Army Force Generation (ARFORGEN) system, designed to provide commanders with a "steady state"—a ready force adequate for the country's needs. That said, new cuts may well push the French army beyond the tipping point. Its next major planning blueprint, a new *Livre Blanc* expected 2013, may show it following the UK's lead by renouncing part of the operational spectrum and compromising on sustainability or readiness. Early indications suggest, however, that the French plan to maintain spending at current levels.

One of the more intriguing aspects of British, French, and German debates regarding the future of their forces is the great extent to which the conflict in Afghanistan and the Lebanon War weigh on the minds of military planners. We found that the Afghanistan mission presents something of a conundrum to these militaries, if not a Rorschach test. It is a stability operation, thus underscoring, for some, the importance of investing in the kind of force structure and capabilities associated with stability operations—especially "softer" skills, such as cultural awareness and psychological operations. As will be discussed later, the UK is arguably using this insight to justify tiered readiness, maintaining light infantry brigades with relatively narrow capability sets, and a greater reliance on reserve forces and civilian skills. Another, and probably more important, take away for the UK is that it intends never to get involved in another mission like that in Afghanistan; the British Army no longer regards the ability to sustain a long deployment as something it needs to possess. In contrast, France concluded from its experience in the Afghanistan mission that its force had become too soft and that, if anything, it had to reaffirm its conventional warfighting skills, even as part of its preparation for stability operations. However, there appears to be tension within the French army regarding the resources required for such a fight. Also, France has been using precision-guided standoff weapons to good effect in recent operations in Libya and Mali while at the same time fielding a fairly large ground force in Mali. As for Germany, it does not appear to have drawn any clear lessons from the Afghanistan mission. There seems to be ambivalence both about what to take away from Afghanistan and about what kinds of fights the German army will face in the future.

This study proceeds country by country, with individual chapters addressing Britain, France, and Germany. Each of these chapters provides an overview of the respective army's response to fiscal austerity and examines its efforts to reorganize its force structure in light of doctrinal debates about the requirements of future warfare. The study relies primarily on British, French, and German government publications; articles by officers in the three countries' militaries; press reporting; and interviews with analysts; it avoids detailed information on specific programs. This study was conducted independently of the research reported in F. Stephen Larrabee and Stuart E. Johnson, et al.'s *NATO and the Challenges of Austerity*.[1] While the two studies share similar conclusions, the present study focuses exclusively on armies as opposed to overall militaries, and it aims to explore in greater depth the thinking behind force structure changes.

---

[1] F. Stephen Larrabee, Stuart E. Johnson, John Gordon IV, Peter A. Wilson, Caroline Baxter, Deborah Lai, and Calin Trenkov-Wermuth, *NATO and the Challenges of Austerity*, Santa Monica, Calif.: RAND Corporation, MG-1196-OSD, 2012.

# 2. Britain

The British Army was already struggling to absorb significant funding cuts while sustaining operations in Afghanistan—a combination that has all but exsanguinated the force. Then, in July 2012, military planners announced not only that the cuts had not gone far enough, but that the scale of the necessary reductions made it impossible to get away with simply trimming the existing force. On the contrary, the planners decided, it was necessary to "go back to first principles" and rethink both the army's mission and the force structure required by that mission. The new plan, referred to as "Army 2020," calls for substantially recasting the British Army's mission, its approach to readiness, and its force structure.

## Scope of Reductions

The cuts called for by Army 2020 follow nearly a decade of struggling to reduce costs while still sustaining operations in Afghanistan. In a sense, the British military as a whole mortgaged its future to pay for the Afghanistan mission. This has important ramifications for the army, not to mention the Royal Air Force and the Royal Navy, which suffered the lion's share of budget cuts over the past decade while the army—because of Afghanistan—was "ring-fenced" and thus relatively spared until recently. The most notable example of the cost of Afghanistan to the long-term well-being of the army is Britain's long-delayed equivalent of the Future Combat System (FCS) vehicle program, known as the Future Rapid Effect System (FRES), which is intended to provide the army with a new generation of medium-weight, networked armored vehicles that will be the backbone of the force for much of this century. One reason for the travails of FRES—which one analyst described as "alive but not quite kicking"—is the diversion of money to the Ministry of Defense's (MoD's) crash program to purchase and upgrade vehicles for use in Iraq and, above all, Afghanistan, where Britain's existing vehicles were found to be dangerously inadequate.[2] According to a study published in May 2011, beginning in 2003, the UK spent approximately £2.8 billion using the Urgent Operational Requirements process to buy and upgrade vehicles for the two theaters of operations.[3] Most of that money went to acquiring Mine Resistant Ambush Protected (MRAP) variants, referred to by the British Army as Protected Patrol Vehicles (PPV). Significantly, despite the great cost of rushing PPVs into service, the MoD considers them to be largely irrelevant for post-Afghanistan operations and unsuitable for

---

[2] Olivier Grouille, "Infantry Equipment: FRES – Alive but Not Quite Kicking," RUSI, June 16, 2009, p. 48.

[3] British Ministry of Defense, *The Cost-Effective Delivery of an Armoured Vehicle Capability*, HC 1029, London: National Audit Office, May 20, 2011, p. 4.

inclusion in the British Army force structure.[4] PPVs, the MoD insists, are simply no substitute for FRES.

A series of planning documents capped by the 2010 Strategic Defense and Security Review (SDSR) offered a vision for a way out of the fiscal hole in which the army found itself and proposed a post-Afghanistan future in which the force would be re-centered and its conventional warfare capability revived, allowing it to more legitimately claim to be FSO capable. The SDSR aimed at reducing the amount of "muscle" the British Army would have to cut and at getting FRES back on track by maximizing savings. The plan called for closing bases, repatriating troops currently garrisoned in Germany, and trimming the military's civilian staff. One innovation in which the British Army placed a great deal of stock was the Whole Fleet Management (WFM) system. The idea behind the WFM system is that, rather than issue a full complement of items to units, some of these items, such as armored vehicles, are kept in a central pool and issued out as required for training and operational purposes.[5] The fleet, moreover, is managed and maintained by private industry. The idea is to save money by reducing the total size of the vehicle fleet required and leveraging private industry's greater efficiency.[6]

Nonetheless, cuts to the force size were unavoidable. The SDSR called for reducing the overall size of the army from roughly 105,000 to 98,000 and shrinking the 400 vehicle–strong main battle tank (MBT) fleet (Challenger IIs) by 40 percent to about 240 and the army's stock of AS90 155mm howitzers by 30 percent.[7] The army was still counting on FRES to be the backbone of the future force, but Britain does not plan to bring it into service until the next decade. One leading British defense blogger describes the FRES program as moving forward yet incoherent and vulnerable to further delays.[8] Indeed, a 2011 study warned that the army would be stuck with an obsolete force of armored vehicles until at least 2024/25, when new vehicles are finally expected to have entered service in significant numbers.[9]

In contrast to the SDSR, Army 2020, announced in July 2012, represents an altogether more radical vision that not only trims the army's capabilities but significantly reduces sustainability and readiness to preserve the remaining capabilities. Army 2020's authors concluded that the SDSR was inadequate, and they called for reducing the size of the army to 82,000 personnel by

---

[4] British Ministry of Defense, 2011, p. 24.

[5] British Ministry of Defense, "Whole Fleet Management Programme Management Office (WFM PMO)," December 19, 2012.

[6] A lengthy discussion thread on the subject of WFM that appears on a British military-related website suggests that there is considerable skepticism regarding the system's performance. See Army Rumour Service, online forum, undated.

[7] HM Government, "Securing Britain in the Age of Uncertainty: The Strategic Defence and Security Review," October 2010, p. 25.

[8] Gabriele, "UK Armed Forces Commentary: CEC Dead, FRES SV Delayed?" *UK Armed Forces Commentary*, May 26, 2012.

[9] British Ministry of Defense, 2011, pp. 6–8.

2015 and dissolving 17 units of different types, as well as five full battalions.[10] Moreover, the army is dividing the force using a system that combines tiered readiness with specialization. FRES is still on the books but is not due to enter service before 2022, and the army plans to bridge the gap by moving ahead with plans to modernize the existing vehicle fleet.[11] Additionally, the MBT fleet is set to shrink to 227 Challenger IIs. All of these numbers add up to one thing: The British Army is officially crossing the threshold beyond which it can no longer be the force it wants to be, which means it cannot be expected to play the role it has in the past and do everything it was once able to do, at least not as well.

## Force Structure and Doctrine

The most salient feature of the British Army's new force structure, aside from its reduced size, is its embrace of specialization and tiered readiness, which ideally will help ensure that its remaining capabilities can still occupy the middle of the conflict spectrum aimed for in the now defunct SDSR. Britain will divide its army into two basic forces, a Reaction Force and an Adaptable Force. There is a third Force Troops force that basically consists of support units available to the Reaction and Adaptable Forces. The Reaction Force consists of three heavy Armoured Infantry Brigades (AIBs)—down from five deployable brigades organized for expeditionary operations—and a single Air Assault Brigade (AAB) "trained and equipped to undertake *the full spectrum of intervention tasks*," which is not entirely synonymous with FSO, given that "intervention tasks" represent a subset of tasks.[12] According to the British military, the Reaction Force will "undertake short notice contingency tasks" and provide "conventional deterrence for defense." It will, moreover, "provide the *basis* for any future enduring operation."[13] This is not the same as being capable of a sustained operation, much less something along the lines of Operation Enduring Freedom in Afghanistan. Indeed, the decrease from five to three expeditionary brigades means that the UK army will have a much thinner rotation base, making extended deployments (as in Afghanistan) impractical.

Each AIB will consist of a single armored cavalry regiment consisting of three "sabre squadrons" equipped with Combat Vehicle Reconnaissance (Tracked) (CVR[T]) armored fighting vehicles (AFVs) (and eventually the FRES SCOUT); a single "Type 56 armoured regiment" with three Challenger 2–equipped sabre squadrons; two armored infantry battalions, with three companies equipped with Warrior infantry fighting vehicles (IFVs); and one heavy protected mobility battalion with three rifle companies mounted on Mastiff MRAPs (and

---

[10] Hopkins, Nick, "Army to Lose 17 Units in Cuts, Defence Secretary Announces," *The Guardian*, July 5, 2012.

[11] Gabriele, "UK Armed Forces Commentary: The Force of Army 2020," *UK Armed Forces Commentary*, September 15, 2012, http://ukarmedforcescommentary.blogspot.com/2012/09/the-force-of-army-2020.html.

[12] British Army, "Transforming the British Army, July 2012: Modernising to Face an Unpredictable Future," July 2012, p. 4.

[13] British Army, 2012, p. 4.

eventually the FRES UV).[14] Within the Reaction Force, there will be something of a force generation cycle, with only one of the AIBs designated the "lead" brigade, while the other two are focused on training and "other tasks."[15]

The Adaptable Force will consist of a pool of seven medium-to-light infantry brigades. Each will include Light Cavalry Regiments with three Sabre squadrons mounted on lightly armored Jackals, Protected Mobility Battalions with three Rifle Companies on new Foxhound light MRAPs, and Light Role Battalions with three rifle companies. Like the Reaction Force, the brigades in the Adaptable Force will cycle through readiness stages, with roughly a third ready and/or committed, a third in training, and a third designated for "individual training/other tasks."[16]

Army 2020 casts the Adaptable Force in a variety of roles. These include meeting the army's "standing commitments," such as garrisoning the Falklands, and meeting UN commitments, as well as "overseas military capacity building" and military support for "homeland resilience." The Adaptable Force will also backfill the Reaction Force in the case of "enduring operations." More intriguingly, the Adaptable Force, which is intended to draw 30 percent of its strength from reserves, is expected to be the repository for "softer" skills associated with stability and homeland operations. Part of the justification for relying on reserves is that such skills often align more with civilian skills than with military ones. Thus, a force that leans heavily on reserve soldiers will, in fact, be better prepared for operations requiring "softer" skills than a force that relies entirely on regular soldiers. While this may be true, at least one British military observer has expressed skepticism about the army's ability to come up with adequate numbers of units, given its preference for going to war with four maneuver units, and he doubts that the Adaptable Force will be able to cobble together the necessary units when called upon.[17] Another reason for skepticism is that the plan requires integrating the reserve and active components to an unprecedented degree, treating the reserves differently, and in effect negotiating a different relationship between British employers and their employees who are reservists.[18]

Although the size of the force is obviously dictated by financial constraints, the precise shape of the force and the compromises it makes in terms of capabilities and readiness reflect a careful evaluation of risk grounded in the hard-nosed assessment of future conflict. Until Army 2020 was established, the British Army was wed to the idea that it needed to be not only capable of the entire spectrum of operations but also retain the capacity for autonomous action at a significant

---

[14] British Army, 2012, p. 5.

[15] British Army, 2012, p. 4.

[16] British Army, 2012, p. 6.

[17] Gabriele, "UK Armed Forces Commentary: The Infantry of Army 2020: Lethality," *UK Armed Forces Commentary*, August 8, 2012.

[18] Louisa Brooke-Holland and Tom Rutherford, *Army 2020*, House of Commons Library, Standard Note 06396, July 26, 2012, pp. 27–28.

scale. For example, the 2008 "Future Land Operational Concept" paper called for maintaining broad capabilities:

> Land forces will need to project suitably configured, scaled and trained forces at appropriate readiness, in order to intervene at a time and place of choice. . . . Land forces need to confront opponents and situations with a broad range of capabilities that retain the ability to conduct sustainable and protracted major combat operations after the required preparation period. . . . Land forces must be capable of major combat, yet be optimized for simultaneous or discrete stabilization tasks.[19]

The MoD's 2010 "Future Character of Conflict" study, conducted in the lead-up to the SDSR, similarly stated that, because the UK will continue to face an uncertain world, involvement in a range of conflicts cannot be ruled out. In other words, the MoD judged that the army had to retain the full spectrum of capabilities as a hedge against uncertainty, although the same study acknowledged "this approach may be challenged by the growing pressure on resources and the increasing span of conflict."[20]

That same year, the SDSR included a blueprint for the British Army known as the "Future Force 2020" (not to be confused with the more recent "Army 2020"). In it, the SDSR called for dividing UK land forces into three tiers. The first tier was a "deployed force," which would consist of Special Forces and a few other elements, such as explosive ordinance disposal units. The second tier was a "high readiness force," which was divided into a light force for "one-off deployments" that would consist of Special Forces and air assault and commando brigades and a "multi-role brigade," reserved for more enduring engagements. The third tier was a "lower readiness force," would consist of four other "multi-role brigades" that would be coming off of deployments or "high-readiness roles" and training and refitting for future activities. This plan amounted to a dynamic force generation system akin to the U.S. Army's ARFORGEN, albeit at a much smaller scale.

One objective stated by the SDSR was to be able to deploy a single brigade of about 6,500 troops with maritime and air support anywhere at any time and sustain it indefinitely while also conducting smaller, short-term operations elsewhere. Alternatively, the SDSR called for the ability to muster a force 30,000 strong for a single, concerted effort with a short time frame. The SDSR also stipulated that British forces be able to act unilaterally, meaning that the army required robust command and control (C2) capabilities, while the Royal Navy and Royal Air Force were expected to be able to move and sustain the army.[21]

---

[19] British Ministry of Defense, 2011, p. 2.

[20] British Ministry of Defense, "Future Character of Conflict," Development Concepts and Doctrine Centre, 2010, p. 1.

[21] HM Government, 2010, p. 19.

With respect to force structure, Future Force 2020 consisted of a series of compromises and wagers intended to ensure that the force retained as broad a swathe of the capabilities spectrum as possible. The first was that, in the face of a bewildering array of possible missions, the optimal choice was a "one-size-fits-all" force that is configured to handle the greatest variety of missions—though its core skillset is ideally appropriate for high-intensity combined arms maneuver warfare—and do so with a high degree of flexibility. The British Army described this compromise as a "return to basics." The army, according to this view, had become too "bespoke" in terms of equipment and capabilities in response to the particular requirements of the Afghanistan mission. Thus, the army, upon leaving South Asia, needed to be reset and shaped into a generic but flexible force designed to handle FSO, particularly combined arms maneuver warfare.[22]

Here we see the influence of the 2006 Lebanon War on British military thinking: According to one analyst, the British Army took from that war the idea that the Israel Defense Forces performed poorly because they were overly specialized and had forgotten how to do old-fashioned combined arms maneuver warfare. In the words of the Ministry of Defense's 2010 "Future Character of Conflict" study, Hizbullah "exploited an Israeli inability to conduct air/land maneuver."[23] From this experience, the army concluded that it was important to maintain a broad range of capabilities, including sufficient firepower.[24] This implied that the army would have to maintain a mixture of light, medium, and heavy forces supported by specialist troops and enablers.

The second major compromise found in the SDSR was the choice of a medium-weight force. The SDSR called for a "balanced force," but the predominant elements in the force structure envisioned by Future Force 2020 were light infantry and motorized elements that would eventually be equipped with the FRES family of medium-armor vehicles; heavy forces, including MBTs and large-caliber artillery, were marginalized to the point where only enough would be maintained to preserve the capability for regeneration if some later contingency required it.

This choice reflected the view that a predominately medium-weight force, tempered with a small but capable MBT element, offers the best "bang for the buck" with respect to firepower, mobility, and protection. A corollary assumption was that MBTs had little role in the kinds of deployments envisaged by MoD planners, or at least not so important a role as to justify the considerable cost of maintaining a large stock of them. The planners' assessment of MBTs was

---

[22] Mark Phillips, "Exercise Agile Warrior and the Future Development of UK Land Forces," RUSI, May 2011, p. 15.

[23] British Ministry of Defense, 2010, p. 19.

[24] Phillips, 2011, p. 17.

not, however, shared by everyone. According to press reports, British commanders in Afghanistan asked for the deployment of Challenger IIs but were refused.[25]

Another compromise was the argument that quality is an adequate substitute for quantity. Indeed, the SDSR explicitly argued for quality over quantity and for "using the minimum number of different equipment fleets, providing both quality and effectiveness."[26] One example of the application of this principle is the SDSR's argument that the use of precision-guided artillery shells will mean that fewer gun tubes are necessary, thus justifying the reduction in the British Army's pool of 155mm howitzers.[27]

In contrast to the SDSR-era plans, Army 2020 assumes greater risk while scaling down the British Army's ambitions. Much of the vision articulated in Army 2020 feels like an attempt to retroactively make the best of a bad situation imposed from outside, much the way a recently laid-off worker might argue that he always wanted to sell the house and move to a smaller apartment because of the greater convenience of apartment living. Nonetheless, the thinking behind Army 2020 is coherent, and it reveals a great deal about how British planners view the state of warfare today and in the foreseeable future, as well as their vision of the UK's role in future conflicts.

According to the principal author of Army 2020, Lieutenant General Nicholas P. Carter, he and his planning team concluded that it was necessary to entirely rethink the army's mission and its requirements and "go back to first principles." What would future conflict look like? What would be the British Army's mission? Which requirements did it need to meet? How ready did the army need to be? The goal was to tailor the army's force structure and approach to force generation and readiness so that they corresponded precisely with the kinds of missions the army thought most probable.

In his recent description of the planning process, Carter began by creating a Venn diagram that laid out the basic requirements of the British Army (see Figure 2.1). The term *contingent capability* refers to warfare. The question is, what kind of warfare? According to Carter, the British Army now sees warfare in terms of a "spectrum of hybrid opponents." As he explained it, at one end of the spectrum are state-sponsored hybrid threats—i.e., Hizbullah in Lebanon in 2006. In the middle of the spectrum are non-state regulars, a category in which he places the Taliban. At the opposite end are non-peer states. Carter argued that the state-sponsored hybrid threats were the most difficult, and he believed that the British Army needed to focus above all on their end of the spectrum.

---

[25] "Tanks 'Needed to Fight Taliban,'" *The Telegraph*, December 19, 2010.

[26] HM Government, 2010, p. 17.

[27] HM Government, 2010, p. 25.

**Figure 2.1. Requirements of the British Army**

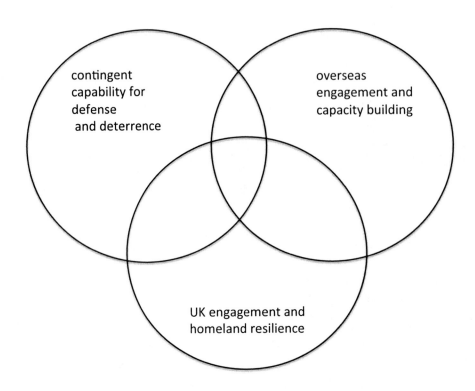

Of note is the fact that Carter's spectrum excludes any possibility of a war against a peer state. In other words, Hizbullah is believed to represent the most difficult opponent the British Army will face. Indeed, according to Carter, while the army still regards tanks as essential, it no longer envisions maneuvering and fighting with tank formations but rather sees them as working in close coordination with small infantry formations. Carter also expressed an interest in cutting back on training that did not require collective training, suggesting that relatively few British units would have the benefit of participating in larger scale exercises. Also noteworthy is the scale of the operations Carter envisioned for the future force, as well as its degree of autonomy. Specifically, Carter said that the army's new force structure is designed with two possible contingencies in mind:

1. A battle-group sized, complex intervention at the same time as a simple intervention and a brigade-level enduring commitment.
2. Three battle-group sized interventions with no concurrent enduring commitment.[28]

---

[28] Lieutenant General Nicholas P. Carter, "British Army 2020: Ground Forces and Future National Security," Center for Strategic and International Studied, September 28, 2012.

Carter described a third contingency—an "all hands at the pump" event in which the army would need to field a division of three brigades—but said the army is not resourced for such an eventuality and is operating under the assumption that the UK would have enough time to react to the emerging situation to provide the necessary resources and ready the required forces. He also made clear that he assumed the UK would only conduct such an operation as part of an international—most likely American-led—operation. In addition, Carter expressed the view that it would be practically guaranteed that a UK division would be reinforced by an outside brigade—probably an American or French unit—acting organically within it. Whereas in the 2010 SDSR the army still imagined the need to field—on its own—a division-sized force, now it has renounced that ambition. According to Carter, this is an acceptable risk.

Carter argued (while this might only be putting the best face on a bad situation) that the army will make up for its small size by being better trained and fighting smarter. One aspect of this is that the force generation cycle will downshift from two years to three, ostensibly to provide more training time; another is the hope that, by relying more on reserves, especially for the Adaptation Force, the army will have the opportunity to leverage the UK's immigrant communities, which can provide unparalleled expertise regarding potential areas of deployment.

*Approach to Readiness*

The British Army is planning to rely on tiered readiness by dividing its force in two. There will now be a "Reaction Force," consisting of three heavy-to-medium weight brigades and one air-assault brigade, which will be kept at a constant state of high readiness, and a second "Adaptation Force," consisting of seven medium-to-light infantry brigades kept at a lower readiness state.[29] The Adaption Force is not, strictly speaking, a reserve force, as Army 2020 calls for elements of the Adaption Force to deploy with the Reaction Force, and there are many missions in which the Adaptation Force is meant to take the lead. Some units in the Adaptation Force might be maintained at higher readiness states than others. It is unlikely, however, that they will be as ready as the Reaction Force, given that they are, by design, undermanned. The plan is for the Adaptation Force's battalions to draw 30 percent of their battle strength from the UK's reserve component, the Territorial army.

Among other things, this scheme means that the Reaction Force units may be the only units that possess conventional fighting skills. In other words, Britain may, in essence, have no more than a small army within an army (i.e., the four brigades permanently assigned to the Reaction Force that are trained, equipped, and ready for a high-intensity fight). The size of the planned battalions is also of concern, particularly with regard to those battalions assigned to the Adaptation Force. As one commentator has pointed out, they will not have enough people to fight the way British infantry units are trained to fight; it is questionable whether the active component will be able to coordinate sufficiently well with the Territorial army to have the

---

[29] Brooke-Holland and Rutherford, 2012, p. 8.

people it needs, with the skills it needs, when it needs them; and there will be little capacity to absorb any attrition or unexpected drop in manning levels.

Finally, according to many observers, the British Army is losing its ability to sustain deployments overseas for any length of time because of inadequate numbers of soldiers and inadequate resources. Three expeditionary infantry brigades is an insufficient force to conduct long deployments.

## Conclusion

Army 2020 has finally forced the British Army, which has been clinging to the idea of being able to field autonomously and sustain a significant FSO-capable force, to bring its ambitions in line with its means. While preserving what might be described as a competent, potent punch in the form of its armored brigades, the army ultimately is reduced to missions that require, at most, a brigade with some additional battalions and a great deal of outside help. From the point of view of managing risk, the British are making a series of bets:

- Medium-weight forces seeded with some heavy armor will suffice for the kinds of high-intensity contingencies they are likely to encounter.
- The UK will not need to quickly muster more than one medium-weight brigade and some portion of light infantry brigades; if more are required, there will be adequate lead time to respond appropriately.
- The UK will not need to sustain even a brigade-sized force for any length of time; there will be no more missions like that in Afghanistan.
- The UK will not have to be involved in a major conflict alone. The UK also seems to expect to get a lot out of its cooperative agreement with France, meaning that it is counting on France to remain roughly as strong as it is.
- The UK will not have to fight a peer country.
- Combined arms warfare is possible but at a relatively limited scale. The most difficult situation the British Army will prepare for is fighting the Second Lebanon War alongside French and/or American forces. It will not plan to fight against peer armored and combined arms forces. As Carter put it, the British Army does not expect to see much corps-level maneuvers in the future.
- The benefits of modernizing the army's vehicle fleet by bringing FRES into service will compensate for the cuts made to finance modernization; quality will compensate for reduced quantity, at least for the types of missions envisioned by British military planners.
- The lighter, less ready Adaption Force will not be committed to a battle it is not prepared to handle without enough lead time to get up to speed.
- WFM will yield significant savings.

The UK will no doubt boast a skilled and professional army that will acquit itself well given any particular task and most likely punch above its weight. However, it will no longer have an army that can deploy or sustain a force anywhere near the size of the British contingents in the

Persia Gulf War and the recent wars in Afghanistan and Iraq. There is arguably also the danger that the UK will be hampered by aging equipment while it waits for its modernization programs to regain lost ground. The British Army will also struggle with the competing demands of modernizing older gear versus investing in new gear.

With regard to lessons for U.S. planners, much depends on how well the British Army approach works out, and it will be some time before the British force structure resembles what is now being envisioned, particularly given the delayed timeline for modernization. At the very least, Carter's cogent analysis of future conflict, particularly with regard to the risk represented by Hizbullah in 2006, merits consideration.

# 3. France

The French army presently is enjoying something of an Indian summer. It still maintains a full spectrum of capabilities—including the capacity for combined arms maneuver warfare—as well as a significant capacity for autonomous and sustained action. However, that may be coming to an end. A new *Livre Blanc* (White Book) that will spell out the army's next steps is expected soon, after several months' delay. Among those steps might be significant cuts. If so, it must be stressed that the French army is already operating at the tipping point. Any further cuts would force the French army to reduce its force structure and capabilities such that it would no longer be able to carry on performing multiple missions at multiple levels of intensity at the same time. Fortunately for the French army, early indications suggest that the French government intends to maintain spending at current levels at least for now. Indeed, France seems an unlikely candidate for the same scale of compromises the British have made for a number of reasons:

- The Afghanistan mission did not significantly affect the French army or derail its modernization efforts.
- Modernization is proceeding as planned and bringing intriguing new capabilities to the force.
- France's considerable overseas commitments and its vision of future conflict support its army's conservative approach to force structure and preparing for high-intensity conflict while sustaining numerous operations abroad.
- France's intervention in Mali appears to have reinforced the perception in the French public and government that the army has to retain its current size and capabilities.

The French army's relative well-being owes itself to a variety of factors. First, it has been spared the kinds of cuts suffered by the British Army. The army budget has remained flat, which amounts to a cut, but one that the army has been able to absorb through a variety of cost-saving measures, including base closures and the adoption of WFM. France's new defense cooperation agreement with the UK also promises some savings for both countries, as demonstrated by France's recent use of British C-17s for operations in Mali, although it remains to be seen how far UK-France cooperation will go and how it might affect either country's ground forces. Second, France did not commit itself to the war in Iraq, and the Afghanistan mission has not strained French resources to nearly the same extent it has the British. France has spent significantly less money on improving vehicles and purchasing MRAP variants for use in Afghanistan, which also means the French army will have a far smaller MRAP fleet to repatriate or otherwise dispose of after it withdraws. France has preferred to make due with its existing vehicle fleet both because it must keep the operational requirements of the army's other missions in mind and because it found its ageing *Véhicule de l'Avant Blindée* (VABs) and AMX-10s to be adequate to the task. This has enabled the French army to stick to its modernization schedule. It will not, for example, have to make significant cuts simply to afford modernization, given that much of the modernization has already been paid for.

Moreover, the French army has been able to hold to a road map for modernization and reform that, though evolving, has remained coherent and remarkably consistent. This modernization process began in 1996 with a move to professionalize the force. It then grew to include an ambitious modernization program akin to the U.S. Army's Future Combat Systems and it culminated with the 2008 *Livre Blanc*, which updated France's vision of its security needs and detailed its future force structure. The 2008 *Livre Blanc* also set in motion the reduction of France's African garrisons in order to make a larger percentage of its force available for a broader range of operations. France has been consolidating its forces, and the fact that the initial deployment to Mali consisted of troops based in France might be indicative of future practice. In other words, French planners have had the luxury of working proactively and deliberately rather than reacting to shifting economic and political conditions or responding to pressing Afghan mission–driven requirements. As a result, the French army has so far escaped having to make difficult decisions about which capabilities to maintain and which to drop. It also retains a vision of future conflict and France's role in the world that calls for a force structure with considerable capabilities, although it remains to be seen how future cuts will affect that vision.

## Scope of Reductions

Cuts to its budget so far have forced the French army to trim its force and pursue a strategy, similar to that in the UK's SDSR, of moving toward a medium-weight force calculated to be optimal for the broadest array of contingencies. Otherwise the cuts have not forced France to compromise its commitment to FSO; autonomous action; and multiple, sustained operations. There are multiple reasons for this. The first is that the budget cuts have so far been light, at least in comparison to those faced by the British and German militaries. The budget has, in effect, grown slightly or remained flat since 2009. For example, the 2011 budget was €31.2 billion, not including pensions, and the 2013 budget is set to be €31.4 billion, without pensions (although, as of June 28, the Defense Ministry has been asked to trim the 2013 budget by seven percent and the 2014 and 2015 budgets by four percent).[30]

Much of the reductions have been paid for through base closures and the sale of property. Also, in 2008 France followed the British lead by introducing its equivalent of WFM, known as *Politique d'emploi et de gestion des parcs* (PEGP), which the French army is optimistic will generate significant savings over time.[31] There also have been cuts to the force. For example, the

---

[30] Pierre Tran, "French Budget Holds Defense Spending Flat," *DefenseNews*, August 2, 2012.

[31] On the French application of WFM, see Commandant C. Bourgeois, Hadrien Hugot, Vincent Legendre, and Laurent Pajou, "La Recherche opérationnelle au service de la politique d'emploi et de gestion des parcs (PEGP)," EURODECISION, 2010; J. Mienville, "Premiers Pas...vers une politique d'emploi et de gestion des parcs (PEGP),"

army reduced its Leclerc MBT inventory to what is considered the minimum number (250) with which effective units can be maintained.[32] It folded the reduced-size Leclerc units, along with heavy artillery, into two relatively heavy armored "brigades de décision," which are basically heavy cavalry units.[33] In addition, according to Philippe Gros, a French military analyst interviewed for this study, the support and logistics elements necessary for deploying and sustaining forces have seen their resources sharply reduced, and throughout the army, broken or worn out parts are not being repaired or replaced at optimal rates, if at all.[34] Another French military analyst, Bastien Irondelle, observed that programs referred to as "operational coherence programs" are often sacrificed, in part because they have no "political" or "industrial" importance.[35] Two examples Irondelle provided are portable bridges and tank transporters.

A source within the French army Command similarly observed that the army's staffing elements have been cut to a point where the army has had to assume some risk. As he explained in an interview, the French army historically has had three levels of staffing: the highest is the "conception" level, which takes place at the French equivalent of the Pentagon; the "conducting level" is performed by the French Armed Forces Command; and the "executing level" is performed by the brigades. Cuts, combined with improved communication, have resulted in reductions at the highest and lowest levels. The middle level has assumed many of the responsibilities of the other levels, both making it more essential and making it its performance more precarious, as there is less slack in the system.[36]

Clearly, the French army has little or no spare capacity, and the precarious arrangement that has enabled the French military to hold together so full a slate of capabilities is unsustainable under the present fiscal conditions. The next cuts may well push France over the tipping point. Moreover, the closure of facilities to save money in accordance with the directives of the *Livre Blanc* comes with an inestimable cost to capabilities. For example, France has closed a number of training facilities, including its mountain warfare school. According to Gros, elements of the mountain warfare training program can and have been transferred to remaining facilities. However, their net quality is not the same in the absence of a dedicated mountain warfare center.[37]

---

*Cavaliers Blindés*, No. 5, November 2006, pp. 2–3; Murielle Delaporte, "Le soutien des forces terrestres en mutation (première partie)," *TTU*, November 2008; and Pierre Tran, "Lt. Gen. Jean-Tristan Verna," *DefenseNews*, May 9, 2011.

[32] Anne-Henry de Russé, *"Transformation" et contre-insurrection: Implications capacitaires pour les forces Terrestres Occidentales*, Focus Stratégique, Laboratoire de Recherche sur la Défense, 2009, p. 36.

[33] de Russé, 2009, p. 36.

[34] Philippe Gros, interview with the author, July 15, 2011.

[35] Bastien Irondelle, interview with the author, June 14, 2011.

[36] Bertrand Darras, interview with the author, September 20, 2012.

[37] Gros, 2011.

Another important reason for the French army's relatively healthy fiscal state is that the Afghanistan mission has affected it far less than other militaries. For example, although we have not obtained data regarding France's off-budget spending to upgrade and purchase new vehicles to meet Afghanistan-specific requirements, it is clear that France has spent far less than the UK. The number of new vehicle types in the French inventory that the army purchased for specific Afghanistan requirements is small: 53 BvS 10 armored personnel carriers (known as Vikings in the British military), 15 Aravis MRAPs, and five U.S.-made Buffalo mine detection and disposal vehicles.[38] This compares with the British Army's 459-strong fleet of Cougar MRAP variants.[39] Moreover, the BvS 10s, known in the French Army as Véhicules à Haute Mobilité (VHM), are intended for general use by its rapid intervention forces, where they will replace older and smaller BvS 206 models. In other words, the army needs the equipment regardless of the Afghanistan mission. The French army has, by and large, made due with its preexisting vehicle inventory, dominated by the venerable VAB and AMX-10. This has enabled the army to stick to its modernization plan of replacing both with new vehicles. Britain, on the other hand, has had to cut its force size to free up enough money to kick-start its flagging FRES program.

## Force Structure and Doctrine

The French army, following the plan laid out in the 2008 *Livre Blanc*, has roughly 130,000 members, and it is structured to be able to deploy 30,000 "in six months for a year . . . disposing of autonomy with regard to their principle combined operations" and with a capability that will "cover the range" from major, short-term operations to long-term stability operations."[40] Short of that, the army is expected to be able to conduct several smaller-scale operations at the same time, including long-term deployments of up to 5,000 troops, while maintaining a 5,000-strong force in reserve in France.[41] The *Livre Blanc* also reaffirms the need for France to be able to conduct small- to medium-scale operations autonomously. French planners do not envision getting involved in a major fight alone.[42]

What currently distinguishes the French army's force structure from that of the British Army is not just the size of the force but its resistance to specialization; its focus on largely conventional capabilities; and its organization around overseas deployments, which, to date, remain a given for French strategy. Although in general terms the French force is a medium one

---

[38] "France," *Jane's World Armies*, March 15, 2013; "France Acquires Vikings to Equip Its Rapid Intervention Forces," *Defense Update*, 2013.

[39] "France," *Jane's World Armies*, March 15, 2013; "France Acquires Vikings to Equip Its Rapid Intervention Forces," *Defense Update*, 2013.

[40] Government of France, *Défense et Sécurité nationale: Le Livre Blanc*, Paris: Odile Jacob/La documentation Française, 2008, p. 211.

[41] Government of France, 2008, p. 200.

[42] Government of France, 2008, p. 200.

that relies on light regiments, the French army remains committed to maintaining conventional warfighting skills within its capabilities balance. As we shall see, the French army took away a surprising lesson from the Afghanistan mission regarding the future of stabilization operations.

The French army is organized into eight maneuver brigades, excluding the light Franco-German Brigade. The brigades can be divided into three categories: heavy (2x), medium (4x), and light (2x). The two heavy armored divisions, which own the army's remaining Leclercs, are intended for high-intensity combat and play the role of torchbearers for combined arms fire and maneuver conventional warfare. According to a French military website, these heavy cavalry brigades will be capable of FSO but will maintain the "unique and essential role of *ultima ratio regum*" because of their "feline" power of "fire and shock."[43] Colonel Bertrand Darras, currently posted with the French Ground Forces Command, observed in an interview that, even though France now has the same number of MBTs as the UK, the French army is not following the British example by "returning to WWI doctrine" and abandoning the idea of massed armor and moving in formation. Darras was referring to the WWI-era employment of tanks primarily to support infantry rather than as independent formations operating under their own command. The French army generally followed this approach on the eve of WWII and suffered poor results against German armored divisions; General Charles de Gaulle famously criticized French tank doctrine and favored larger, independent formations.

The bulk of the force, however, will consist of four light-to-medium–weight "multirole brigades" built around the new *Véhicule blindé de combat d'infanterie* (VBCI) and *Véhicule blindé multi-rôles* (VBMR), which are intended to replace the AMX-10P IFV and the VAB Armored Personnel Carrier (APC), respectively. The vehicles in these brigades will be wheeled, which in itself represents a set of compromises with regard to firepower, mobility, and protection based on the gamble that the benefits of a lightened logistics burden and greater air deployability will outweigh the disadvantages.[44] According to a source in the army, the turn to wheeled vehicles should be seen as no more than a concession to deployability, for he suggested that the army would otherwise prefer tracked vehicles.

Both the VBCI and the VBMR are part of the French army's modernization program referred to as SCORPION (*Synergie du Contact Renforcé par la Polyvalence et l'infovalorisation* [System of Contact Reinforced by Versatility and Information]), which resembles the U.S. Future Combat Systems program, particularly in terms of its emphasis on commonality and leveraging information technology. The new vehicles are designed to be fully networked and act as hubs connecting a variety of networks. At the squad level, soldiers equipped with personnel communications and networking gear known as FÉLIN (*Fantassin à Equipements et Liaisons Intégrés* [Infantry Soldier with Integrated Equipment and Networks]) are networked with one

---

[43] *Ultima ratio regum*, or "last argument of kings," was the motto Louis XIV had cast on his cannon. French Ministry of Defense, "La Brigade De Décision," Centre De Doctrine d'Emploi Des Forces, undated.

[44] de Russé, 2009, p. 36.

another and with the vehicle from which they dismounted, while vehicles are networked to one another, to larger formations, and to ground and air-based fire support.

The 25-ton VBCI—which comes in two basic models, a standard vehicle and a command vehicle—is now in service and has been deployed to Afghanistan. According to *Jane's International Defense Review*, the VBCI's Battlefield Management System (BMS) and communications links greatly enhance situational awareness, speed up planning and task execution, and make it possible for VBCI formations to conduct tactical maneuvers without being within visual range of one another.[45] Also according to *Jane's International Defense Review*, French commanders have already noted an important challenge posed by the VBCI's technology, which is that making full use of its capabilities requires a better trained, higher-quality crew than the AMX-10P. In particular, the gunner, who commands the vehicle in the standard VBCI model, must be adept at directing fires and coordinating with other vehicles and the FÉLIN-equipped dismounts to make full use of the BMS.[46]

The VBMR family is still in development, but, as of this writing, remains on time to enter production by 2015, with a total planned purchase of as high as 2,300, all variants included (see Table 3.1). Of course, the schedule and the size of the planned purchase may change as a consequence of the recently mandated budget cuts. The VBMR vehicles, all built upon common, modular bodies, will include heavy (20-ton) six-wheeled and light four-wheeled scout variants mounting a variety of weapons and gear. The requirements include the ability to add as much as five tons of additional armor.[47] Of course, the VBMR will feature the same BMS and communications systems as the VBCI.

### Table 3.1. France's Future Armored Vehicle Fleet

| | | |
|---|---|---|
| Leclerc (in service) | MBT | 250 |
| VBCI (in service) | IFV | 630 |
| VBMR (production planned for 2015) | APC | 2,300 |

NOTE: Does not include the significant numbers of modernized AMX-10s and VABs that will remain in the inventory for the remainder of the decade.

FÉLIN itself represents a major advance. Like the VBCI, it has already been fielded in Afghanistan and is being progressively introduced throughout the army. The gear consists of a suite of high-tech components, including a helmet, helmet-mounted optics and LED displays, a gun site and gun-mounted video camera, a computer display, communications gear (osteo-

---

[45] Rupert Pengelley, "High-performance VBCI Makes New Demands on French Infantry Training," *Janes International Defense Review*, May 11, 2009.

[46] Pengelley, 2009.

[47] "SCORPION, the Future French Hybrid Warfare System Solution," *Jane's International Defense Review 2011*, May 10, 2010.

microphone and vibrating speaker, voice and data links), and a battery pack. The system links soldiers to one another, as well as to the armored vehicles with which they are operating their BMS (France has been upgrading the old VABs with new BMS computers and communications systems while the army waits to replace the VAB with the VBMR). The French army's experience with operating FÉLIN in the field has yet to be made known, beyond general comments that it works very well, particularly with respect to allowing units to communicate in near silence and operate well at night. However, an article in *Jane's International Defense Review* about a joint UK/French exercise highlights two new problems that arose from FÉLIN: technical interoperability difficulties between the French and UK networks and the need to bridge the gap between British and French Tactics, Techniques, and Practices, which, the article implies, is growing as the French learn to work with FÉLIN.[48] Nonetheless, a French Foreign Legion officer who has not had personal experience with FÉLIN noted in an interview that the army has already had enough experience with FÉLIN for it to have evolved: Operational experience has led to the shedding of components and capabilities that were found to be unnecessary or impractical. Colonel Darras added that the system could benefit from being more lightweight and from improved ergonomics with respect to both the equipment and its software.

Despite the French army's division of the force between heavy brigades earmarked for conventional warfare and lighter units, as well as its progress with SCORPION, it should be stressed that the French army is less willing than the British Army to assume that quality can make up for a loss in quantity, and it is anxious to avoid specialization. For instance, the *Livre Blanc* states, "the criteria of numbers . . . remain pertinent and cannot be entirely compensated for with quality.[49] Elsewhere it argues that, "Even if weapons develop all of the qualities that have been predicted, number remains a determinant factor for most operations, whether they take place on the ground, on the sea, or in the air . . . the capabilities that armies possess represent a reasonable compromise, intended to provide a sufficient number of soldiers, sailors, and aviators quality material."[50] As retired Lieutenant General Vincent Desportes, arguably France's leading military thinker, said in a radio interview in 2011, the premise of using high technology to offset cuts in numbers is false, since, in practice, what ends up happening is that numbers get cut to afford the technology.[51] That is indeed what the British have done.

One of the reasons for France's approach to the quality versus quantity debate is a strong critique of the U.S. military's concepts of "transformation" and "effects-based" warfare.[52] French

---

[48] Rupert Pengelley, "France Brings FELIN to the UK," *Jane's International Defense Review*, March 5, 2012.

[49] Government of France, 2008, p. 130.

[50] Government of France, 2008, p. 203.

[51] "Général Vincent Desportes," *L'Invité du jour*, Paris: France Culture, February 2, 2011.

[52] For a good overview of the French debate over "transformation" and other current doctrinal issues, see Joseph Henrotin, "Adaptation et contre-adaptation au défi du caractère évolutif de la guerre. Un aperçu des débats français," *Les Cahiers du RMES*, Vol. 5, No. 1, 2008, pp. 131–163.

military thinkers, including retired Colonel Michel Goya and, most importantly, Desportes, whose last command was France's Joint War College, have argued that the "transformation" approach to warfare is useless against conventional opponents because it is based on too many false assumptions about the nature of the conflict and the nature of the opponent. They find evidence for this position in the Lebanon War, as they see the Israeli military that went to war in 2006 as one heavily influenced by U.S. doctrine and configured to conduct two things: (1) "transformation" warfare using very expensive stand-off precision strike capabilities and (2) special operations adapted to counterinsurgency and counterterrorism activities. Neither of these things, according to French analysts, provided an adequate substitute for an infantry-led combined arms maneuver campaign. Moreover, French analysts, including Desportes and Goya, assess that transformation warfare completely misses the mark in any kind of population-centric mission, such as counterinsurgency or stabilization operations, where destroying things and killing people often aggravates the situation, and tactical victories are practically irrelevant.[53]

Desportes, in particular, has argued that the modern reliance on stand-off strike capabilities does not correspond with the kind of conflict one faces today, in which the real objectives are not tactical or even military, but political and social.[54] In an editorial in the French military publication, *Doctrine*, for example, Desportes argues that all military operations need to be regarded as communications operations in which it is absolutely necessary to control the environment. That requires a presence on the ground of large numbers of troops over a long period of time. He states, "We have understood that, contrary to the false evidence that is too commonly shared, number is a quality in itself; we have understood that fire power is indispensable but cannot compensate for too few men."[55] In 2007, Desportes testified to the French Senate that "the point of warfare is not to destroy, but to control," and "if [one] cannot control the ground," one has not achieved anything. To establish control, he continued, "there has been only one solution for as long as the world has been the world . . . if you want to control, you have to be present in number in the physical environment where crises are born, grow, and settle themselves, which is to say on the ground." "Ask our American and Israeli friends, who now know something about this."[56] These comments predate the missions in Libya and Mali, and it remains to be seen to what extent those operations have influenced French thinking.

Both Desportes and Goya have even argued in favor of fielding lower-technology weapons if it would allow the army to field greater numbers of soldiers and invest in their training, provided

---

[53] Henrotin, 2008, pp. 131–133, 140–141; Michel Goya, "Dix millions de dollars le milicien: La crise du modèle occidental de guerre limitée de haute technologie," *Politique Étrangère*, No. 1, 2007, p. 198.

[54] Vincent Desportes, "Editorial," *Doctrine: Revue d'Études Générales*, No. 13, 2007a, p. 3.

[55] Desportes, 2007a, p. 3.

[56] Vincent Desportes, "Forces terrestres et nouvelle conflictualité," *Doctrine Tactique: Revue d'études générales*, No. 13, 2007b, p. 6.

the weapons are not so obsolete as to make the force ineffective.[57] Desportes goes so far as to suggest finding a creative two-tiered arrangement in which the United States pursues high-tech forces while its North Atlantic Treaty Organization (NATO) allies opt for a lower-tech military that is at least large enough to be useful.[58] Similarly, the Legionnaire interviewed for this study expressed concern that the French army had learned some bad lessons in Afghanistan with regard to fighting "American-style warfare" in the sense that infantrymen worked in conjunction with drones, satellites, and fast jets providing close air support on demand. France could not afford to fight like that, he said, and besides, it was contrary to the experience of most French officers, who often have to operate in the field with few resources.

This attitude is all the more striking given the progress of the French army's Future Combat Systems programs, such as FÉLIN, which embody the technologies associated with "transformation." Indeed, according to Bastien Irondelle, French commanders are ambivalent about FÉLIN and fear that it will fuel the perception that quality is a substitute for quantity.[59] Also, France has made good use of precision-guided strike capabilities in Libya and Mali, suggesting that France is not about to abandon its stand-off precision weapons. Colonel Darras, in fact, cautions against assuming that Desportes and Goya represent the mainstream opinion in the French army. Among other things, he said, the argument in favor of a large but lower-tech force runs counter to France's aversion to casualties, which is one of the main drivers behind its embrace of precision, stand-off weaponry.

With regard to specialization, the French insist it is not a good idea. There are two parts to the French argument. The first is quite simply that, given the range of possible missions, what France needs most is a flexible FSO-capable force. The stress is on adaptability. "This permanent capability of adaptation," argues the *Livre Blanc*, "explains why France does not choose to specialize its forces but aims instead for flexibility." "France must have," the *Livre Blanc* continues, "an intervention capability that is flexible and reactive, capable of conducting the entire spectrum of operations, often with the same men."[60]

The second aspect of France's argument against specialization is the conviction that, despite France's heavy involvement in stability operations, ultimately what its army needs to focus on is the conventional end of the conflict spectrum, regardless of whether its units are heavy, medium, or light. As noted earlier, Israel's experience in Lebanon confirmed thinkers like Desportes in their view that conventional combined arms maneuver warfare skills remain essential. Surprisingly, the Afghanistan mission, for the French, has provided the same lesson.

According to Darras, the French army had always thought of itself as a force that focused on conventional "major combat operations," even though it spent most of its time involved in

---

[57] Goya, 2007, p. 201.

[58] Vincent Desportes, "Armées: 'Technologisme' ou 'juste technologie'?" *Politique Étrangère*, No. 2, 2009, p. 417.

[59] Irondelle, 2011.

[60] Government of France, p. 130.

stability operations. Moreover, it initially treated the Afghanistan mission as another stability operation, meaning in practical terms that the troops it deployed there as part of the International Security Assistance Force (ISAF) mission in Kapisa Province were prepared no differently than those sent to Côte d'Ivoire. The Sarobi District massacre of 2008, however, in which ten paratroopers died, brought home the painful realization that the army had, in effect, become a stability operations force despite its self-image as a conventional force, meaning that, when faced with the level of violence encountered in Afghanistan, French soldiers who might do fine in Africa were in serious jeopardy. According to Darras, whereas the U.S. military had to learn to lower its reliance on fires and brute force in Afghanistan, the French army found that it needed to do the opposite and bring more violence to the fight.

In practical terms, one of the measures enacted by the French army following Sarobi was to change the way it prepares its forces for deployment to Afghanistan. Rather than treat it as just another overseas deployment, the French army invests heavily in providing troops destined for Afghanistan with more extensive and realistic mission-specific training. Some of that training consists of the "softer" skills one might expect for a counterinsurgency mission. However, according to Darras, a lot of it consists of more advanced conventional warfighting training to ensure that French troops who find themselves in another situation like Sarobi will prevail. Looking toward the future, Darras said he believes some of the Afghanistan-specific training— presumably the conventional skills—will be retained and perhaps built into the core curriculum. In the view of the French army, future conflicts will require those skills.

Given the French interest in maintaining the force at its present size, the question remains as to how the French army will be able to sustain its commitment to the full spectrum of capabilities in the event of future cuts. One indication of how the French army might attempt to strike a compromise can be found in Desportes' vision of future conflict. Desportes makes clear that future conflict is most likely going to come in the form of stabilization operations, and he stresses the need for the French military to be able to adapt to the exigencies of population-centric warfare.[61] However, the army is not to do this by developing the capacities required for stability operations and thus investing less in conventional warfighting skills, but rather by knowing when to stop fighting and hand the reins over to nonmilitary government agencies better suited for stabilization. The military's job is no more and no less than killing or deterring whoever might seek to interfere with the efforts of other actors to improve the quality of life of local populations. To that end, the military needs to focus on ensuring it can outmatch any foe. In other words, it is to remain essentially a conventional force, although not necessarily one focused on fighting other nations.

---

[61] Desportes's views on the nature of future conflict and the army's role in it can also be found in FT-01, which is France's equivalent to the U.S. Army's FM 3-0. See French Ministry of Defense, *Gagner la bataille, Conduire à la paix: les forces terrestres dans les conflits aujourd'hui et demain*, FT-01, Centre de Doctrine d'Emploi des Forces, 2007.

## Approach to Readiness

The French army operates a five-stage force generation cycle akin to the U.S. ARFORGEN, built around four-month deployments and the basic requirement that two brigades always be available, one of which must be a medium or heavy brigade, so that army commanders have some choice regarding how big a hammer to apply to a particular situation. Within the system, there is some flexibility regarding the length of training time, as well as an important surge capacity, which relies on making sure those units that are midway through their training are nonetheless sufficiently practiced in their conventional warfighting skills to be safely dispatched to most missions.

The French force generation cycle begins with a period of post-deployment leave and reset and then proceeds through two training stages, each punctuated by rotations through France's national training centers. First is a core course built around a standard set of warfighting skills. According to Darras, those skills are not defined as a formal set of what the U.S. Army refers to as Mission Essential Tasks but nonetheless are fairly uniform. Units who reach a certain phase within this stage of their training are regarded as an available surge force, known as *Guépard* (Cheetah). Commanders facing a contingency thus have the option of directing elements from the two operational brigades or tapping *Guépard* for the mission. The next phase of training is tailored for units' assigned missions, known as *Mise en condition avant projection* (MCP), or Pre-Deployment Training. Troops at this stage of training are not available for *Guépard*. The length and resources invested in MCP vary according to the assigned mission. Afghanistan-bound units are given the highest priority, and the army spares little expense, making their training as rigorous, complete, and realistic as possible. According to Darras, prior to Sarobi, the army did not provide this extra level of training. In fact, the troops killed in 2008 were *Guépard* and thus drawn from the same pool of forces French commanders routinely tap for African missions. The MCP curriculum offered to units heading for Afghanistan combines more-advanced training in conventional warfighting skills—so that troops can handle spikes in violence—as well as theater-specific expertise, including cultural training and exercises in mock Afghan villages. In the meantime, savings are sought elsewhere: Troops not destined for Afghan deployments receive less-specialized training, much of it consisting, in effect, of on-the-job training provided by the commanders responsible for France's many deployments, which range from homeland security operations to counter–illegal mining operations in the jungles of French Guyana and various duties in Africa. In the future, Darras argued, much of the Afghanistan-specific training will be built into the core curriculum, specifically the more-advanced combat training that enables even those troops on stabilization operations to respond appropriately to significant spikes in violence.

## Conclusion

The French military is in the relatively enviable position of having been sheltered from major budget reductions while operating in Afghanistan at a scale that has not drained its resources. As a result, the distance between the French army's aspirations for full-spectrum capabilities and operational autonomy is narrow when compared with the British Army. That said, there is little to no slack available to the army, and whether it can sustain itself at its current funding levels, let alone absorb larger cuts, is debatable. Darras insists that the army will never give up its efforts to modernize the force. However, one must wonder how it can afford to field new vehicles at the same time that it tries to preserve the size of the force. The publication of a new *Livre Blanc* may provide an answer.

There is an important qualitative side to the story that will emerge more fully in the comparison made later between the French military and the German military: Behind France's commitment to full spectrum operations is a vision of its army as a warfighting force that it routinely uses to advance the country's interests. The French army is active around the globe and is not shy towards violence. As Darras points out, the army's high operational tempo and frequent overseas deployments is not only a given for the force but part of its appeal: That's what people sign up for. So long as the French army sees itself as a warfighting institution, it will do what it can to remain a warfighting institution.

France, for now, could repeat its contribution to ISAF and probably go beyond that, if required. What is more intriguing for U.S. and NATO planners, however, is that France is well in advance of Britain with regard to fielding the kind of medium-weight, high-tech force that both countries aspire toward. Early indications—though information is scarce—have been positive both with respect to France's Afghanistan deployment and mission in Mali, where France has been coordinating air and ground offensives and deploying both precision-guided strike weapons and basic infantry tactics. Although the situation in northern Mali is unlikely to be a repetition of what happened in southern Lebanon in 2006, it will nonetheless test France's new equipment, as well as its army's thinking regarding the military's role in future conflicts, the balance required between stand-off weapons and "boots on the ground," and the trade-offs between quality and quantity. The mission in Mali should also test France's force generation system, its ability to sustain troops, and its post-Sarobi confidence that it is generating troops who are "ready enough."

# 4. Germany

The German military, perhaps more than even the British military, faces a period of profound uncertainty. Although it cannot be described as drained of resources in the same manner as the British military, the German military has been subject to a series of deep cuts while being buffeted by the shifting winds of German politics and economic conditions, all without the British or French army's sense of purpose. The German military is committed to a full spectrum of capabilities and has been going through a number of reforms intended to change its force structure, primarily to make it more like the French army, that is, more *einsatzfähig* (usable, or, literally, capable of operating) and expeditionary, while at the same time reducing its overall size. Unlike the French, however, the Germans appear to put much less emphasis on remaining capable of conventional combined arms maneuver warfare, and—again in contrast to the French—the Afghanistan mission appears to have made the Germans more conflicted regarding the prospect of high-intensity combat. Thus, despite protests to the contrary and a force structure that will maintain enough armor to mount the same kind of punch as the British and the French, the Germans appear to be sliding toward a force geared primarily toward stabilization operations of a less violent nature than those contemplated by the others. This is, in part, a result of German military theorists' conception of future conflicts, as well as a result of the way *Grundgesetz* (German Basic Law or Constitution) prescribes specific roles to the German military. The post-war German allergy to military conflict appears to be fading, but Germans find it hard to imagine themselves performing militarily other than as part of a multinational deployment operating under the mandate of the United Nations, the European Union, or NATO.

## Scope of Reductions

In the spring of 2011, Germany set out to cut its defense budget by €8.3 billion by 2015.[62] Planners have hoped to cover most of that sum by closing several hundred military facilities and cutting the overall size of the military from roughly 228,000 airmen, sailors, and soldiers to "up to 185,000."[63] According to the German military's website, as of October 2012, the total size of the military had dipped just below 200,000.[64]

While many of these cuts have fallen on the Navy and the Air force, the size of the army has declined from just over 100,000 at the end of 2010 to 70,000 in October 2012, according to the

---

[62] Sebastian Fischer, Matthias Gebauer, and Philipp Wittrock, "Streichen, Kürzen, Schrumpfen," *Spiegel Online*, May 18, 2011.

[63] "Weniger U-Boote, Weniger Panzer, Weniger Kampfjets," *Spiegel Online*, April 22, 2011.

[64] German Ministry of Defense, "Die Stärke der Streitkräfte," October 12, 2012.

German military's website and *Jane's*.[65] The German army is reducing its force from five divisions to three, and from eleven brigades to eight, according to its website.[66] Its fleet of Leopard 2 MBTs will shrink from 350 to 205 and the number of Puma IFVs will go from 405 to 350, according to *Jane's*.[67] Despite the cuts, German planners hope to increase the size of the force the German military is capable of deploying and sustaining indefinitely from 7,000 to 10,000.[68] According to *Jane's*, this translates into increases in the German army's light infantry forces. army aviation will also be cut: The CH-53 fleet will be transferred to the Air Force and new helicopters will be procured in significantly smaller numbers than planned. There will be only two transport helicopter regiments with 40 NH-90s each, and only one Tiger attack helicopter regiment equipped with 40 Tigers. There has also been an effort to find efficiencies by reorganizing various aspects of the military, dissolving administrative levels, and letting go large numbers of civilian employees. The German army also appears to be moving toward a WFM-type structure, with the expectation that it will yield considerable savings and allow the army to purchase fewer Leopards and smaller Puma and Boxers.[69] Indeed, in a June 2012 German army publication, *Info-Brief Heer*, Lieutenant General Bruno Kasdorf makes it clear that the army is aiming for the "minimal requirements" with regard to major weapon systems (see Table 4.1).

**Table 4.1. Germany's Future Armored Vehicle Fleet—Minimal Objectives**

| | | |
|---|---|---|
| Leopard 2 (in service) | MBT | 225 |
| Puma (in service) | IFV | 350 |
| Boxer (in service) | APC | 684 |

SOURCE: Kasdorf, 2012, p. 2.
NOTE: Does not include the significant numbers of modernized Marder IFV and Dingo APCs that probably will remain in the inventory for the remainder of the decade.

Arguably the single most important change affecting the German army is the decision in 2010 to abandon conscription and professionalize the military. While the move should result in a more capable force that is also more readily deployed abroad—primarily because the army would not or could not deploy conscripts overseas—it raises the cost of recruitment by an unknown amount, as the military will have to raise salaries and spend money on advertising and various incentives to encourage young Germans to volunteer. Also, conscription gave the German military the opportunity to identify conscripts it wanted to encourage to enlist after the term of conscription had expired. Early indications are that the German military faces an uphill

---

[65] German Ministry of Defense, ; "Germany," *Jane's World Armies*, March 8, 2013.

[66] Frank Bötel, "Ausblick: Die Bundeswehr der Zukunft," Bundeswehr, September 3, 2012.

[67] "Germany," *Jane's World Armies*, March 8, 2013.

[68] German Ministry of Defense, "Eckpunkte für die Neuausrichtung der Bundeswehr," May 18, 2011.

[69] Bruno Kasdorf, "'Durchhaltefähigkeit—Modernität—Attraktivität': Prinzipien für die Struktur HEER2011," *InfoBrief Heer*, Vol. 17, No. 3, June 2012, p. 5.

battle winning over young Germans. Now that the last class of draftees has entered the ranks, the military is concerned that it will be unable to fill its recruitment quotas.[70] It might conceivably be a hollow force for at least the next few years.

## Doctrine and Force Structure

While being forced to absorb major budget cuts, the German military has been in the throes of a significant effort to transform its force structure so as to recast itself from a Cold War legacy force geared toward a defensive land war in Europe to an expeditionary force. This is the theme that runs throughout the official German defense policy papers since at least the 2006 *Weissbuch* (*White Book*) and the purpose of the most recent wave of reforms proposed by the 2010 Weise Commission Report and expanded on by Minister of Defense Karl-Theodor zu Guttenberg prior to his resignation in March 2011. Again and again, one finds in these documents the wish for the army to become more *einsatzfähig*.

In effect, what this means is that the German army wants to be more like the British and French forces. It too is moving toward a medium-weight force based on new IFVs and APCs (the Puma and Boxer, respectively), which, like the French VBCI and VBMR, are designed to take full advantage of information networks. Among other things, they are designed to work with the FÉLIN-like suit of personnel gear referred to until recently by the program name *Infanterist der Zukunft* (Infantryman of the Future), or IdZ, and now known as Gladius. The German army has just begun entering Gladius into service with an initial order of 900 units, and Gladius-equipped troops are slated to deploy to Afghanistan in 2013–2014. The German army, like the French army, will also retain two heavy armored units, which ostensibly will retain some capability to conduct conventional warfare.

Still, given the scope of the German budget cuts and the army's small target size, it is clear that the German army will have to make considerable compromises with regard to the spectrum of capabilities. It seems improbable that it will be able to hold on to the full spectrum as long as the French have. Significantly, in official publications and statements in the media, high-ranking army officers and other officials insist on keeping the army FSO-capable. As the German equivalent to Field Manual 3-0, the *Heeresdienstvorschrift* (HDv) 100/100, published in 2007, puts it, "the army must be able to fulfill its mission in the entire task spectrum."[71] Yet the way these various documents discuss the spectrum and future conflict makes it clear that, willingly or not, the army is heading toward the lighter end of the spectrum.

The debate has focused around the question of how to prepare troops for Afghanistan. The German army clearly places priority on preparing for the requirements of the Afghan mission, while at the same time acknowledging the need to be mindful of the rest of the "capability

---

[70] "Freiwillig Zum Bund? Nein, Danke!" *Spiegel Online*, April 21, 2011.

[71] German Ministry of Defense, "HDv 100/100 VS-NfD: Truppenführung von Landstreitkräften," 2007, § 8.

spectrum," both with respect to equipment and training. In the words of Lieutenant General Carl-Hubertus von Butler, "a particular challenge is, on one hand, covering the entire breadth of the spectrum and, on the other, focusing on training for a particular operation."[72]

One of the answers adopted recently by German planners was to divide the army into units with different specialties in a manner not unlike what the British are now planning. The idea, first detailed in the Ministry of Defense's 2004 *Konzeption der Bundeswehr* (*Military Concept*) and confirmed by the 2006 *Weissbuch*, was to divide the army into "Intervention Forces" and "Stabilization Forces." The *Weissbuch* also added a "Support Forces" category. The Intervention Forces—built around a single armored division (*Panzerdivision*, or PzDiv)—are intended to prepare for high-intensity conventional operations; they would, according to the HDv 100/100, have the best equipment.[73] In contrast, the Stabilization Forces—comprising two divisions, one mechanized infantry and one armored infantry—have been earmarked for low-to-middle–intensity operations and intended to be able to conduct peacekeeping and stability operations for a long period of time (see Table 4.2). Thus, sustainability would take precedence over firepower for the Stabilization Force. That said, the Stabilization Forces are supposed to be sufficiently equipped and trained to handle spikes in violence and perform well throughout the entire intensity spectrum, which is the reason HDv 100/100 cites for including mechanized infantry among designated Stabilization Forces. As of 2009, at least one of the divisions assigned to the Stabilization Forces, the 13. *Panzergrenadierdivision* (PzGren), included 88 Leopard 2A5s in its inventory.[74]

### Table 4.2. Comparative Sizes of Intervention and Stabilization Forces

|                   | Intervention Force |        | Stabilization Force |        |
|-------------------|--------------------|--------|---------------------|--------|
| Major components  | 1. PzDiv           | 18,000 | 10. PzDiv           | 12,000 |
|                   |                    |        | 13. PzGren          | 12,500 |
| Total             |                    | 18,000 |                     | 24,500 |

What HDv 100/100 and other official documents left unsaid is that Stabilization Forces would be less well equipped than Intervention Forces and thus provide the German military with significant savings. According to Thomas Wiegold, planners in fact hoped that, by giving the Stabilization and Support units cheaper and less-capable equipment, they could provide the

---

[72] Carl-Hubertus von Butler, "Die Zukunft Des Feldheeres: Einsatzorientiert, Führungsstark, Von Werten Getragen," *InfoBrief Heer*, Vol. 15, No. 1, 2010, p. 4.

[73] German Ministry of Defense, 2007, p. 108.

[74] Reinhard Kammerer, "13. Panzergrenadierdivision: Die Division Im Osten Deutschlands" ["13th Mechanized Infantry Division: The Division in Eastern Germany]," in *Heeresführungskommando*, Sankt Augustin: CPM Communication Presse, 2009, p. 57.

Intervention Forces with the latest and most capable equipment. Thus, although in 2009 the 13. PzGren possessed Leopard 2A5s, the 1. PzDiv (1st Armored Division)—the heavy core of the Intervention Forces—was equipped with the more recent Leopard 2A6M, a heavier tank with greater mine protection.[75] Of course, a "less well equipped" German force might still be more than adequately equipped—a Leopard 2A5 is an excellent tank by any measure—but the practice of issuing older or lower-quality kits to certain units might, over time, create other problems, either because the gap between the two forces grows or because the assessment of what is acceptable for a stabilization force proves wrong.

As it happened, both kinds of forces (minus the Leopards) were deployed to Afghanistan, where the Stabilization Forces proved to be deficient with respect to training and equipment. They are simply too light, not to mention too few.[76] Moreover, the military did not fully embrace the plan, and the overlap evident in descriptions of actual units within the Intervention and Stabilization Forces suggest the absence of a coherent doctrine defining the two force structures and their use. The approach has been judged a failure, and according to one source, the German MoD formally rejected it in 2011, although it appears to remain in vigor.[77]

In the aftermath of the failed attempt at force specialization, the question of how the German army intends to balance its capabilities remains open. There remains an ostensible commitment not just to FSO but also to the conventional end of the capabilities spectrum. According to the May 2011 "Defense Policy Guidelines," "in light of the ongoing and unpredictable imponderables [of future conflicts], the military must continue to dispose of a broad and flexible capability spectrum."[78] Lieutenant General Kasdorf, in June 2012, stressed that the army was preparing itself for stability operations but "naturally" must maintain the ability to defend the country and treaty partners.[79] Yet Kasdorf's statement betrays a clear prioritization of capabilities associated with overseas stability operations over those required for conventional combined arms maneuver warfare.

Moreover, there appears to be an important cultural difference born out in the way German military officials talk about the full spectrum. The difference originates with Germany's *Grundgesetz* and the peculiar legal framework within which Germany's post–World War II military operates. As the HDv 100/100 spells out at the opening of its section on operations, the German military can only go to war to defend the nation, rescue citizens, or fulfill its treaty

---

[75] Markus Kneip, "Die 1. Panzerdivision [1st Armored Division]," in *Heeresführungskommando*, Sankt Augustin: CPM Communication Presse, 2009, p. 44.

[76] Timo Noetzel and Martin Zapfe, "Force Structure Requirements for Complex and Conventional Operations: The Case of the Bundeswehr," in Christopher M. Schnaubelt, ed., *Complex Operations: NATO at War and on the Margins of War*, Rome: NATO Defense College, 2010, pp. 146–149.

[77] Thomas Wiegold, interview with the author, July 21, 2011; Martin Zapfe, personal communication, July 11, 2011.

[78] German Ministry of Defense, "Verteidigungspolitische Richtlinien," May 18, 2011b, p. 15.

[79] Kasdorf, 2012, p. 2.

obligations. It can never act abroad unilaterally—except to rescue citizens—and it must deploy as part of a multinational coalition operating with a full United Nations, European Union, or NATO mandate. The German parliament has to approve all deployments.[80] Although German military publications give a nod to the hypothetical possibility that the military might have to get involved in a conventional war in defense of a follow member of NATO or the European Union, the military's legal restrictions and the lack of plausible conventional threats to Germany or its NATO and European allies make the prospect of engaging in a high-intensity symmetrical war unlikely. In contrast, the requirements of Afghanistan are pressing, and the need to prepare for future involvement in multinational stability operations is easy to embrace.

One result is a reluctant embrace of Afghanistan as the German military's most compelling model. For example, Lieutenant General Kasdorf has written of the need in Afghanistan of a professional infantry that is comfortable using the most advanced technology while navigating the myriad cultural and political challenges and struggles that take place among and for control over local populations. Thus Afghanistan, he writes, "is for all the allies and partners the most challenging operation."[81] Yet, he insists, "the operation in Afghanistan is not the blueprint for the future of our army either with regard to the length of the operation or the relevant capability spectrum of the army, that in the face of the diversity of . . . threats must clearly be broader."[82] The army, after all, has to be prepared for its commitments to defend the alliance. Nonetheless, Kasdorf returns to the example of the Afghanistan mission, which he argues provides key insights about the hybrid character of future operations.

Kasdorf's views amount to an argument that, ultimately, the German army's priority needs to be preparing for the next stabilization operation. His perspective is consistent with German military policy. For example, the *Weissbuch 2006* argues for full-spectrum capabilities but also makes it clear that "conflict prevention and crisis management, including the struggle against international terror, are for the foreseeable future [the German military's] probable tasks. . . . They significantly determine and shape the capabilities, management systems, availability, and equipment of the German military."[83] Next, the *Weissbuch* states that the military must *also* (i.e., secondarily) be able to defend allies from attacks, as well as defend German territory, implying that those are the hypothetical scenarios in which other capabilities would be required.[84] Similarly, the May 2011 "Defense Policy Guidelines" describes the two poles of the "entire

---

[80] German Ministry of Defense, 2007, pp. 73–74.

[81] Bruno Kasdorf, "Einsatz, Doktrin und Ausbildung: Auszüge aus der Rede Generalleutnant Bruno Kasdorf Anlässlich Info-Lunch FKH Am 9, June 2011," *InfoBrief Heer*, Vol. 16, No. 3, 2011, p. 2.

[82] Kasdorf, 2011, p. 2.

[83] German Ministry of Defense, *Weißbuch 2006: Zur Sicherheitspolitik Deutschlands und zur Zukunft der Bundeswehr*, Online Ausgabe, 2006, p. 64.

[84] German Ministry of Defense, 2006.

intensity spectrum" as "observation missions" and *"preventative security precautions."*[85] The use of that euphemism—which is a far cry from the bravado of the French army's description of the mission of its heavy cavalry brigades as *"ultima ratio regum"*—mirrors the difficulty with which German planners conceive of getting involved in a conventional war. Moreover, whereas the French took away from their experience in Afghanistan the notion that preparing for stability operations needed to include preparation for a hot fight, the Germans, having been bloodied and drawn blood in South Asia, are reluctant to draw the same conclusions. A case in point is the ongoing debate in Germany over arming airborne drones. In brief, the German military wants armed Predators or similar platforms, but neither the Government nor the public is comfortable with the idea, with public officials taking stands on whether or not such things are ethical.[86] Finally, what emerges is an increasingly weak German commitment to the high-intensity end of the capabilities spectrum. The German army is, perhaps despite itself, well on its way toward becoming a force geared toward stabilization.

## Approach to Readiness

The German army has also attempted to institute a force generation structure akin to the U.S. Army's ARFORGEN. According to the German system, a single division would be responsible for providing the forces required for all deployments for a period of a year, after which it would cycle through two years of reset and training intended to provide both core combined arms maneuver capabilities for high-intensity conventional war and whatever other capabilities are thought to be required for the anticipated future deployment. Interestingly, the Germans treat units going through the system as interchangeable, regardless of whether they belong to the Stabilization rather than the Intervention Forces. For example, the 13. PzGren and the 1. PzDiv have alternated roles as the "lead division" responsible for overseas deployments, even though the former has a lighter force structure than the latter.[87] Both ostensibly are trained for full-spectrum operations, but what is not clear, particularly given the criticism of the Stabilization Forces' ability to handle combat in Afghanistan, are the relative proportions of time and resources dedicated to preparing forces for stability operations compared with combined arms maneuver warfare. According to a description of the 13. PzGren published by its commander in 2009, its training included everything from highly specialized skills relating to stability operations and training for high-intensity conventional warfighting.[88] The description focused more on the stability operations training, however, suggesting that the conventional skills received comparatively less emphasis. However, the language of the description does not

---

[85] German Ministry of Defense, 2011b, p. 15.

[86] Thomas Wiegold, "'Schutz am Boden' statt 'Terror aus der Luft,'" *Augen Geradeaus!*, October 30, 2012.

[87] Kammerer, 2009, p. 58.

[88] Kammerer, 2009, p. 58.

necessarily match the reality. In any case, according to Thomas Wiegold, the German army is abandoning the triennial training cycle because it was determined that, since it was only sending soldiers to Afghanistan on 4-month deployments, the cycle could not be sustained.[89] There simply were not enough troops.

## Conclusion

Germany, like the UK and France, is officially committed to preserving full-spectrum capabilities in the face of sharp budget cuts, and it is doing so, in part, by moving to a medium force structure built around new families of medium armor. The German military is focusing its resources on making itself more deployable and sustainable. It is also emphasizing modernization for two stated reasons: (1) The army is counting on quality to make up for quantity (quality is partially understood to include the virtue of adaptability [e.g., multipurpose gear], as well as professional soldiers with long enlistment terms), and (2) it is convinced that modern equipment will help make the force attractive to new recruits and to soldiers who are already signed up. However, although on paper the German force structure resembles that of France and the UK, with their largely medium-weight forces, the Germans appear to be tilting more toward the lower end of the intensity spectrum. The difference has less to do with weapon systems—Pumas and Boxers resemble VBCIs and VBMRs—than with the cultural and political differences that appear to inform priorities.

The problems the Germans encountered when fielding their relatively light Stabilization Forces in Afghanistan should give pause to planners contemplating specialization, as the British have recently done. As the French, too, learned in Sarobi, the capabilities required for stability operations can be easily underestimated.

---

[89] Wiegold, 2011.

# 5. Conclusion

Successive budget cuts driven by fiscal considerations rather than changes in the security environment have forced Europe's three largest and most capable armies to scramble to find ways to maintain their commitment to the full spectrum of capabilities while compromising on size, sustainability, and readiness. Possessing the full spectrum of capabilities has arguably evolved into more of an ideal or an aspiration than a reality, as British, French, and German armies are increasingly obliged to make compromises based on their assessment of risk and their effort to arbitrate among competing priorities. Moreover, they have reached the point where there is no more fat to cut; the knife now finds only bone and muscle. To maintain as capable a force as possible, the three armies are calculating that having smaller, less sustainable, and, to some degree, less ready forces represents an acceptable risk.

The British Army is in the worst state of the three, owing to the strain that the Afghanistan and Iraq missions have placed on its resources at the same time it has been subject to successive budget cuts. The army judges that it can best meet future exigencies in spite of greatly reduced numbers by dividing the force into a somewhat FSO-capable conventional force and a force geared toward stability operations and bridging this division with a tiered readiness system reliant on reserves. The UK is gambling that it will not have to mount a large operation or sustain an operation, and that it will not have to do so autonomously. In the process, it hopes to occupy as much of the middle of the spectrum of capabilities as possible while also being able to finance the modernization of its medium-weight armored vehicles.

The French army has been less affected by the Afghanistan mission and budget cuts, which has enabled it to charge ahead with modernization while clinging to its commitment to FSO capabilities, including combined arms maneuver warfare. The French have been cutting support and logistical elements, which might render the army's capabilities weaker than they appear on paper, but otherwise its force size and force generation system provide commanders with what they consider to be adequate numbers of ready troops. The publication of a new *Livre Blanc* may alter the situation, however, particularly given how little there is left to cut before the French are forced to make more significant compromises.

One important difference between the French approach thus far and the British approach is that the French are reluctant to substitute quality for quantity, suggesting that, in the future, the French would opt for less-capable but cheaper weapons and equipment if that would allow them to maintain the military's size.

The German military faces significant budget cuts at the same time that it is in the midst of profound reforms and restructuring intended to make its army more expeditionary while maintaining full-spectrum capabilities. The most important reform is the end of conscription, however the army is also following the general trend of shifting toward a medium-weight force based on new medium armored vehicles.

Despite the German military's stated commitment to full-spectrum capabilities, the evidence suggests that it is evolving into a force geared primarily toward meeting the requirements of stabilization operations in general and Afghanistan in particular. Arguably, this evolution has more to do with German culture and politics than it does German military planners' assessment of future conflicts or the highly capable equipment in the army's inventory.

Altogether, we make the following general observations, some of which are contradictory:

- The British, French, and Germans all hold it necessary to be capable of full-spectrum operations, given the unpredictable nature of future conflict.
- The three armies have so far opted to reduce their force size rather than cut major capabilities; reduced force size necessarily affects sustainability, even as units are made more deployable.
- The British, French, and Germans are concentrating on making their militaries as expeditionary as possible and are, to that end, attempt to grow or preserve the size of their operational forces while sharply reducing the size of their generating forces and other support elements. This, too, makes deployments less sustainable.
- The British and Germans are willing to substitute quality for quantity, whereas the French prefer not to do this and appear to regard the current force size as having reached a bottom limit.
- The 2006 Second Lebanon War has had a chilling effect, at least on the British and French, and checked the impetus to move decisively away from conventional capabilities. The war has also led planners to second-guess the ideas of "transformation," with its emphasis on precision-guided stand-off strike, and "information dominance" as substitutes for mass and core joint and combined arms warfighting skills, even as they are cutting mass (at least in the British and German cases) and introducing transformation-associated technologies.
- The UK, France, and Germany are investing heavily in networked warfare to connect individual soldiers with their squads, their medium-weight armored vehicles, and larger networks. France has already deployed these systems to Afghanistan; Germany is expected to deploy them next year. This suggests that, however skeptical they might be about transformation, they still see some value in substituting quality for quantity. France is favoring precision weapons and airpower in Mali, at least in the opening days. Casualty aversion might play a role.
- France is the most committed to high-intensity combined arms maneuver warfare. Its "stick to the basics" approach found validation in Afghanistan, where the French army concluded that even stabilization operations were likely to feature spikes in the intensity of violence and that soldiers needed to be well grounded in conventional warfighting skills.
- All three forces are trending toward medium-weight armored vehicles that are presumed to provide the most "bang for the buck" and cover the greatest range of the spectrum of operations. However, France and Germany are at least a decade ahead of the UK with respect to modernization. Germany has experimented with dividing its force into two weight-classes, each destined for operations of different intensities. The British have

embraced a more radical specialization scheme that relegates stabilization operations forces to a secondary readiness tier. France refuses to specialize and prefers instead to provide some soldiers with additional training depending on their assigned mission.

- All three forces are counting on WFM to yield significant savings both in terms of cutting long-term lifecycle costs and in terms of reducing the numbers of new vehicles they need to purchase.

These observations have multiple implications for the U.S. Army and NATO. First, to state the obvious, the leading European military powers—the UK in particular—cannot be counted upon to sustain anything more than a brigade-sized force, if that. Second, France alone appears to be capable of autonomous action like that occurring in Mali, and France is also arguably the best suited of the three countries for taking on a conventional conflict required combined arms maneuver warfare, as well as less intense stability operations. All this may change as a result of the next French defense budget if it includes further cuts to the army.

More intriguing are European efforts both to define and occupy a "sweet spot" with respect to medium-weight forces based on a new generation of medium-weight armored vehicles that integrate transformation-associated technologies. These new vehicles and their attendant high-tech gear represent

1. a gamble with respect to risk and future conflicts
2. a gamble that quality will, to a significant extent, compensate for quantity.

Both wagers are reasonable ones to make. What might prove them wrong, besides a conflict with a peer military power, is a Lebanon war scenario in which medium-weight forces come up short against a hybrid opponent because they prove too light, or a scenario in which there are simply not enough troops, either because of the requirements of a particular conflict or because there are too many simultaneous conflicts. It is also possible that Britain, France, or Germany might find that its military capabilities are incommensurate with its policy objectives. It will be interesting to see how the UK adapts to having a greatly reduced army, and how France reacts to the prospect of a greatly reduced army. In any case, U.S. military planners can benefit from European thinking about the requirements of future conflicts, as well as their efforts to define priorities. At the very least, the Europeans' experimentation with "transformation" technologies and WFM merit investigation.

# Bibliography

Army Rumour Service, online forum, undated. As of March 12, 2013:
http://www.arrse.co.uk/weapons-equipment-rations/1323-whole-fleet-management-wfm-good-bad.html

Bötel, Frank, "Ausblick: Die Bundeswehr der Zukunft," Bundeswehr, September 3, 2012. As of March 12, 2013:
http://www.bundeswehr.de/portal/a/bwde/!ut/p/c4/04_SB8K8xLLM9MSSzPy8xBz9CP3I5E
yrpHK9pPKUVL3ikqLUzJLsosTUtJJUvbzU0vTU4pLEnJLSvHRUuYKcxDygoH5BtqMiA
MTJdF8!/

Bourgeois, Commandant C., Hadrien Hugot, Vincent Legendre, and Laurent Pajou, "La Recherche opérationnelle au service de la politique d'emploi et de gestion des parcs (PEGP)," EURODECISION, 2010.

British Army, "Transforming the British Army, July 2012: Modernising to Face an Unpredictable Future," July 2012.

British Ministry of Defence, "Future Character of Conflict," Development Concepts and Doctrine Centre, 2010.

British Ministry of Defence, *The Cost-Effective Delivery of an Armoured Vehicle Capability*, HC 1029, London: National Audit Office, May 20, 2011.

British Ministry of Defence, "Whole Fleet Management Programme Management Office (WFM PMO)," December 19, 2012. As of March 12, 2013:
http://www.mod.uk/DefenceInternet/AboutDefence/WhatWeDo/EquipmentandLogistics/WF
M/

Brooke-Holland, Louisa, and Tom Rutherford, *Army 2020*, House of Commons Library, Standard Note 06396, July 26, 2012. As of March 12, 2013:
www.parliament.uk/briefing-papers/SN06396.pdf

Brown, Nick, "France Seeks Armour Upgrade," *Janes International Defense Review*, February 4, 2013.

Carter, Lieutenant General Nicholas P., "British Army 2020: Ground Forces and Future National Security," Center for Strategic and International Studied, September 28, 2012. As of March 12, 2013:
http://csis.org/event/british-army-2020-ground-forces-and-future-national-security

de Russé, Anne-Henry, *"Transformation" et contre-insurrection: Implications capacitaires pour les forces terrestres occidentales*, Focus Stratégique, Laboratoire de Recherche sur la Défense, 2009.

Darras, Bertrand, interview with the author, September 20, 2012.

Delaporte, Murielle, "Le Soutien des forces terrestres en mutation (première Partie)," *TTU*, November 2008.

Desportes, "Editorial," *Doctrine Tactique: Revue d'études générales*, No. 13, 2007a, p. 3.

———, "Forces terrestres et nouvelle conflictualité," *Doctrine Tactique: Revue d'études générales*, No. 13, 2007b, pp. 4–6.

———, "Armées: 'Technologisme' ou 'juste technologie'?" *Politique Étrangère*, No. 2, 2009, pp. 403–418.

Fischer, Sebastian, Matthias Gebauer, and Philipp Wittrock, "Reform der Bundeswehr: Streichen, Kürzen, Schrumpfen," *Spiegel Online*, May 18, 2011. As of March 12, 2013: http://www.spiegel.de/politik/deutschland/0,1518,763419,00.html

"France," *Jane's World Armies*, March 15, 2013. As of March 25, 2013: https://janes.ihs.com/CustomPages/Janes/DisplayPage.aspx?DocType=Reference&ItemId=+ +++1319225&Pubabbrev=JWAR

"France Acquires Vikings to Equip its Rapid Intervention Forces," *Defense Update*, 2013. As of March 25, 2013: http://defense-update.com/20091223_viking.html

"Freiwillig zum Bund? Nein, danke!" *Spiegel Online*, April 21, 2011. As of March 12, 2013: http://www.spiegel.de/schulspiegel/abi/0,1518,758641,00.html

French Ministry of Defense, "La Brigade de Décision," Centre de Doctrine d'Emploi des Forces, undated. As of March 12, 2013: http://www.cdef.terre.defense.gouv.fr/a_la_une/01_2010/Brigade_decision.htm

French Ministry of Defense, *Gagner la bataille, Conduire à la paix: les forces terrestres dans les conflits aujourd'hui et demain*, FT-01, Centre de Doctrine d'Emploi des Forces, 2007.

Gabriele, "CEC Dead, FRES SV Delayed?" *UK Armed Forces Commentary*, blog post, May 26, 2012. As of March 12, 2013: http://ukarmedforcescommentary.blogspot.com/2012/05/cec-dead-fres-sv-delayed.html

———, "UK Armed Forces Commentary: The Infantry of Army 2020: Lethality," *UK Armed Forces Commentary*, blog post, August 8, 2012. As of March 12, 2013: http://ukarmedforcescommentary.blogspot.com/2012/08/the-infantry-of-army-2020-lethality.html.

————, "UK Armed Forces Commentary: The Force of Army 2020," *UK Armed Forces Commentary*, blog post, September 15, 2012. As of March 12, 2013:
http://ukarmedforcescommentary.blogspot.com/2012/09/the-force-of-army-2020.html.

"Général Vincent Desportes," *L'Invité du jour*, Paris: France Culture, February 2, 2011. As of March 12, 2013:
http://www.franceculture.com/emission-l-invite-du-jour-general-vincent-desportes-2011-02-02.html

German Ministry of Defense, *Weißbuch 2006: Zur Sicherheitspolitik Deutschlands und zur Zukunft der Bundeswehr*, Online Ausgabe, 2006.

German Ministry of Defense, "HDv 100/100 VS-NfD: Truppenführung von Landstreitkräften," 2007.

German Ministry of Defense, "Eckpunkte für die Neuausrichtung der Bundeswehr," May 18, 2011a. As of March 12, 2013:
http://www.nato.diplo.de/contentblob/3151176/Daten/1320160/VM_deMaiziere_180511_eck_DLD.pdf

German Ministry of Defense, "Verteidigungspolitische Richtlinien," May 18, 2011b.

German Ministry of Defense, "Die Stärke der Streitkräfte," October 12, 2012. As of March 12, 2013:
http://www.bundeswehr.de/portal/a/bwde/!ut/p/c4/DcmxDYAwDATAWVgg7unYAugc8kSWI4OMIesTXXm002D8SeWQy7jRStshc-4p94L0hENCnXEGUvXXSuMKG8FwBd26TD9uIZiT/

"Germany," *Jane's World Armies*, March 8, 2013.

Government of France, *Défense et Sécurité Nationale: Le Livre Blanc*, Paris: Odile Jacob/La documentation Française, 2008.

Goya, Michel, "Dix millions de dollars le milicien: la crise du modèle occidental de guerre limitée de haute technologie," *Politique Étrangère*, No. 1, 2007, pp. 191–202.

Gros, Philippe, interview with the author, July 15, 2011.

Grouille, Olivier, "Infantry Equipment: FRES – Alive but Not Quite Kicking," RUSI, June 16, 2009.

Henrotin, Joseph, "Adaptation et contre-adaptation au défi du caractère évolutif de la guerre. Un aperçu des débats français," *Les Cahiers du RMES*, Vol. 5, No. 1, 2008, pp. 131–163.

HM Government, "Securing Britain in the Age of Uncertainty: The Strategic Defence and Security Review," October 2010.

Hopkins, Nick, "army to Lose 17 Units in Cuts, Defence Secretary Announces," *The Guardian*, July 5, 2012. As of March 12, 2013: http://www.guardian.co.uk/uk/2012/jul/05/army-lose-17-units-cuts

Irondelle, Bastien, interview with the author, June 14, 2011.

Kammerer, Generalmajor Reinhard, "13. Panzergrenadierdivision: die Division im Osten Deutschlands" ["13th Mechanized Infantry Division: The Division in Eastern Germany]," in *Heeresführungskommando*, Sankt Augustin: CPM Communication Presse, 2009, pp. 56–59.

Kasdorf, Bruno, "Einsatz, Doktrin und Ausbildung: Auszüge aus der Rede Generalleutnant Bruno Kasdorf Anlässlich Info-Lunch FKH Am 9, June 2011," *InfoBrief Heer*, Vol. 16, No. 3, 2011.

———, "'Durchhaltefähigkeit—Modernität—Attraktivität': Prinzipien Für Die Struktur HEER2011," *InfoBrief Heer*, Vol. 17, No. 3, June 2012, pp. 1–5.

Kneip, Markus, "Die 1. Panzerdivision/1st Armored Division," in *Heeresführungskommando*, Sankt Augustin: CPM Communication Presse, 2009, pp. 44–49.

Larrabee, F. Stephen, Stuart E. Johnson, John Gordon IV, Peter A. Wilson, Caroline Baxter, Deborah Lai, and Calin Trenkov-Wermuth, *NATO and the Challenges of Austerity*, Santa Monica, Calif.: RAND Corporation, MG-1196-OSD, 2012. As of March 12, 2013: http://www.rand.org/pubs/monographs/MG1196.html

Mienville, J., "Premiers pas vers une politique d'emploi et de gestion des parcs (PEGP)," *Cavaliers Blindés*, No. 5, November 2006, pp. 2–3.

Noetzel, Timo, and Martin Zapfe, "Force Structure Requirements for Complex and Conventional Operations: The Case of the Bundeswehr," in Christopher M. Schnaubelt, ed., *Complex Operations: NATO at War and on the Margins of War*, Rome: NATO Defense College, 2010, pp. 134–151.

Pengelley, Rupert, "High-performance VBCI Makes New Demands on French Infantry Training," *Janes International Defense Review*, May 11, 2009.

———, "France Brings FELIN to the UK," *Jane's International Defense Review*, March 5, 2012.

Phillips, Mark, "Exercise Agile Warrior and the Future Development of UK Land Forces," RUSI, May 2011.

"SCORPION, the Future French Hybrid Warfare System Solution," *Jane's International Defense Review 2011*, May 10, 2010.

"Tanks 'Needed to Fight Taliban'," *The Telegraph*, December 19, 2010. As of March 12, 2013: http://www.telegraph.co.uk/news/worldnews/asia/afghanistan/8212290/Tanks-needed-to-fight-Taliban.html

Tran, Pierre, "French Budget Holds Defense Spending Flat," *DefenseNews*, August 2, 2012. As of March 12, 2013: http://www.defensenews.com/article/20120802/DEFREG01/308020003

———, "French Put Extra Funds into Support, Ops, in Stable 2013 Budget," *DefenseNews*, September 28, 2012. As of March 12, 2013: http://www.defensenews.com/article/20120928/DEFREG01/309280003

———, "Lt. Gen. Jean-Tristan Verna," *DefenseNews*, May 9, 2011. As of March 12, 2013 : http://www.defensenews.com/story.php?i=6442452&c=FEA&s=INT

von Butler, Generalleutnant Carl-Hubertus, "Die Zukunft des Feldheeres: Einsatzorientiert, Führungsstark, von Werten getragen." *InfoBrief Heer*, Vol. 15, No. 1, 2010, pp. 1–4.

"Weniger U-Boote, Weniger Panzer, Weniger Kampfjets," *Spiegel Online*, April 22, 2011. As of March 12, 2013: http://www.spiegel.de/politik/deutschland/0,1518,758644,00.html

Wiegold, Thomas, interview with the author, July 21, 2011.

———, "'Schutz am Boden' statt 'Terror aus der Luft,'" *Augen Geradeaus!*, October 30, 2012. As of March 12, 2013: http://augengeradeaus.net/2012/10/schutz-am-boden-statt-terror-aus-der-luft/

Zapfe, Martin, personal communication, July 11, 2011.